6 Skills to expand your English

Stretch

3B

Susan Stempleski
Presenting skills consultant:
Ben Shearon

STRETCH

Stretch teaches listening, speaking, reading, writing, viewing, and presenting skills to prepare you for success in academic and professional life.

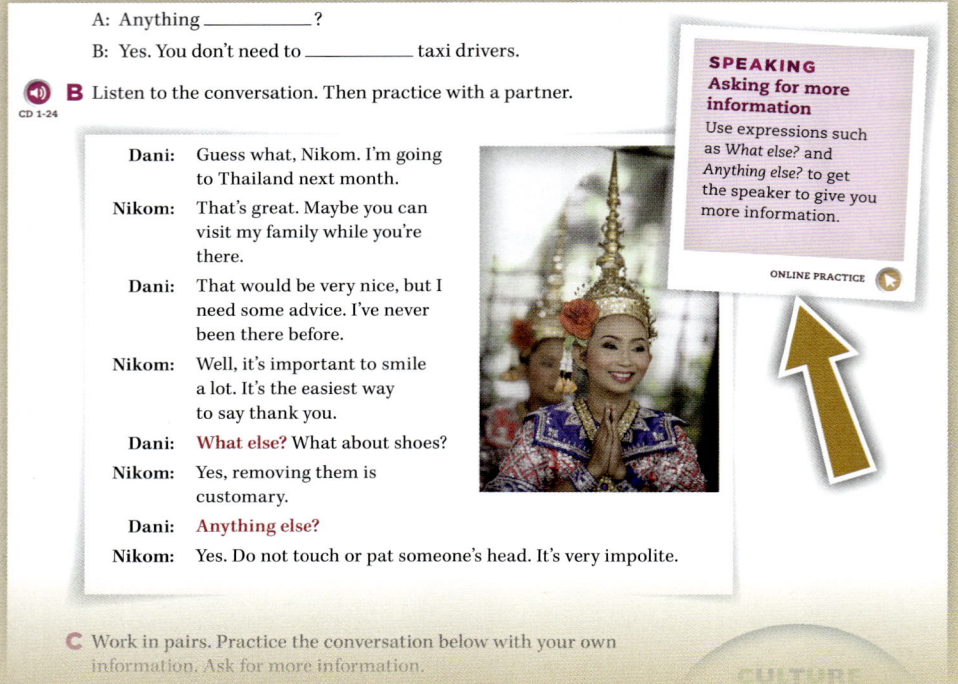

Skill Snapshots

are short presentations that highlight the skills taught in *Stretch*. You can find them on most of the Student Book pages. Skill Snapshots ensure you know what you are learning on each page.

Online Practice

deepens your understanding of the information in the Skill Snapshots by providing new presentations for each of the six skills. You will find more than 100 activities you can do any time, anywhere—with automatic grading and feedback on your answers.

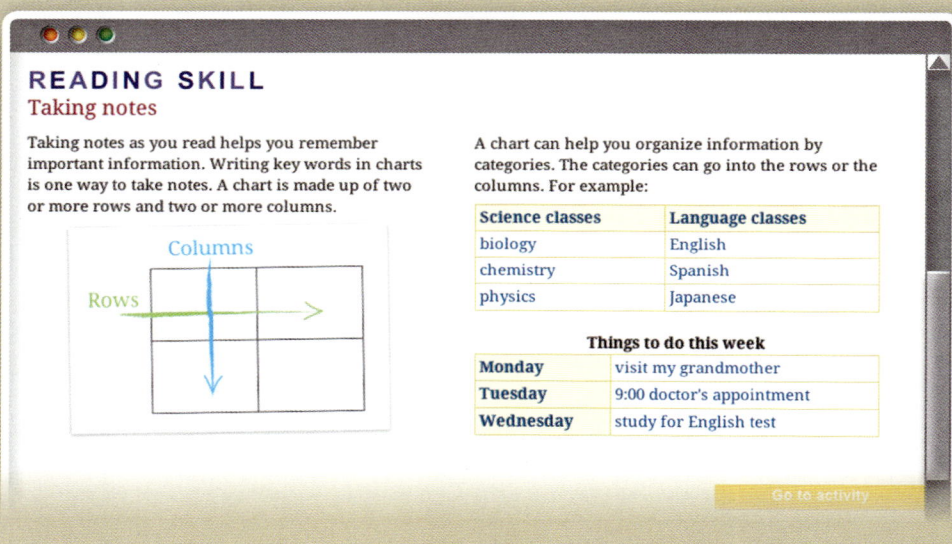

Use the access code on the inside back cover to log in at **www.oxfordlearn.com/login**.

6 Skills to expand your English

Viewing Skills
Research shows that learning English through videos helps you remember more information, develop cross-cultural awareness, and expand your critical thinking. Viewing Skills, such as interpreting facial expressions, use BBC Worldwide Learning videos to teach media literacy for 21st-century success.

Presenting Skills help you become a better public speaker. *Stretch* teaches four types of presenting skills:
1) controlling your body language
2) organizing your ideas
3) designing your message
4) using speech techniques

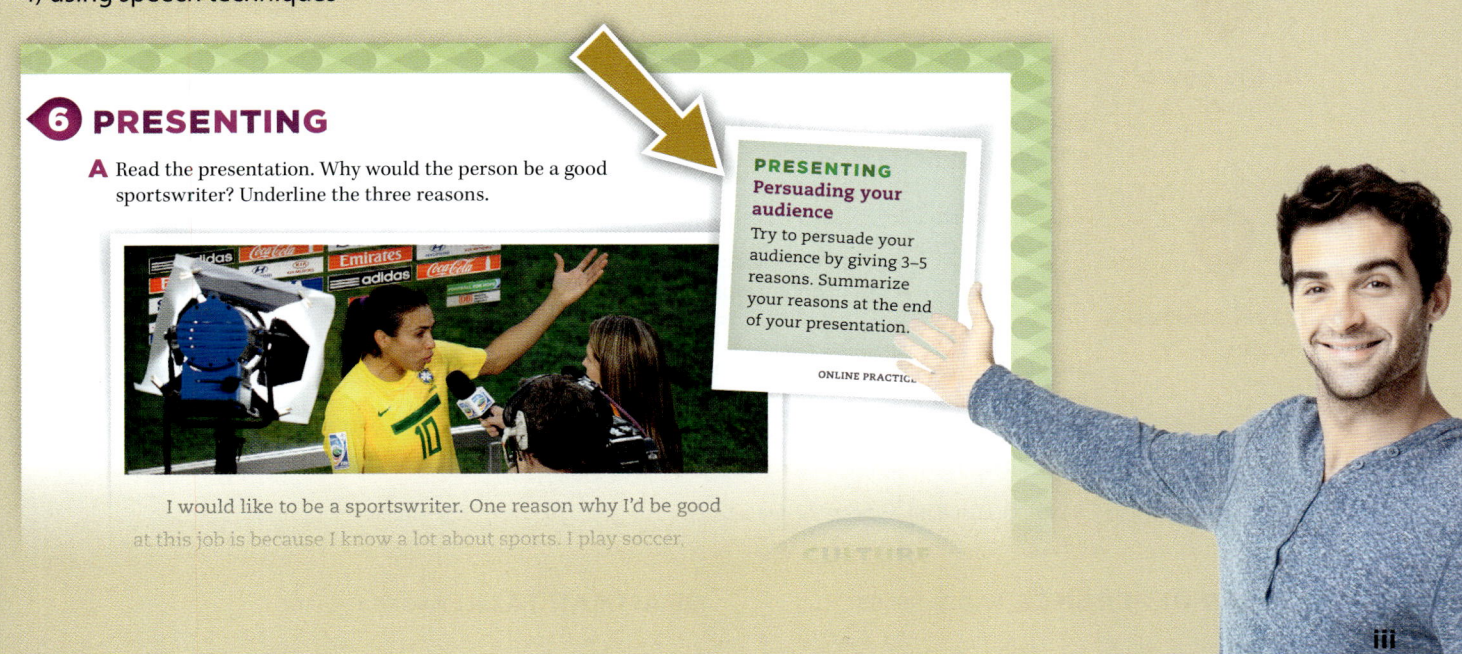

SCOPE AND SEQUENCE

UNIT	VOCABULARY AND LISTENING	SPEAKING	GRAMMAR	READING AND WRITING
7 **Leisure time** Pages 42–47	catch up with friends, build a website, have brunch, etc. **SKILL:** Predicting content	Interesting activities Pronunciation: Reductions of *have* **SKILL:** Adding information	Present perfect continuous and present perfect	Reading: *Social media updates* Writing: *An activity you've been doing lately* **SKILL:** Scanning
8 **Appearance** Pages 48–53	bald, beard, scruffy, etc. **SKILL:** Listening for descriptive words	Changes in appearance Pronunciation: Consonant clusters with *s* **SKILL:** Using phrases to agree	*Used to*	Reading: *High School Reunions* Writing: *Describing someone who has changed* **SKILL:** Making a cluster diagram
9 **Habits** Pages 54–59	get up early, do chores, catch up on the news, etc. **SKILL:** Listening for frequency words	Early life Pronunciation: Past tense endings **SKILL:** Asking open questions	Simple past, present perfect, and present perfect continuous with *How long*	Reading: *At Home on the Water* Writing: *A classmate's life or job* **SKILL:** Using context clues
Self-Assessment Units 7–9 Pages 60–61	Vocabulary and Grammar Reading: *Just Jack: Remembering the Past*			
10 **Stories** Pages 62–67	mystery, biography, historical fiction, etc. **SKILL:** Asking yourself questions	Asking for someone's time Pronunciation: Plural nouns **SKILL:** Refusing politely	Reported speech	Reading: *The Voyages of Zheng He* Writing: *A book review* **SKILL:** Summarizing
11 **In the news** Pages 68–73	flood, election, exhibition, etc. **SKILL:** Listening for main ideas	Waiting for someone Pronunciation: *Let* vs. *late* **SKILL:** Explaining your reasons	*While* and *when* clauses	Reading: *Ricochet the SURFice™ Dog* Writing: *An interesting news event* **SKILL:** Identifying cause and effect (2)
12 **Travel stories** Pages 74–79	lose your wallet, call room service, miss a flight, etc. **SKILL:** Listening for key words (2)	Bad travel experiences Pronunciation: Stress with content words **SKILL:** Continuing the conversation	Present perfect for experiences	Reading: *Travel Mishaps* Writing: *A trip that went wrong* **SKILL:** Self-assessing
Self-Assessment Units 10–12 Pages 80–81	Vocabulary and Grammar Reading: *Lost Ring Appears 72 Years Later*			

GRAMMAR REFERENCE PAGES 88–93　　　　**GRAMMAR TALK!** PAGES 100–105

VIEWING BBC Worldwide Learning	PRESENTING	CULTURE TALK!	LEARNING OUTCOMES I can...
Chinese opera star **SKILL:** *Identifying purpose*	Interesting activities **SKILL:** *Introducing a topic with images*	Dangerous activities Collecting autographs	...add information to continue a conversation. ...scan information in a text. ...introduce a topic with images.
Stuart's new look **SKILL:** *Making predictions*	Before and after **SKILL:** *Focusing on key points*	Makeover TV shows High school reunions	...listen for descriptive words about appearance. ...can ask and answer questions with *used to*. ...make predictions about what I'm going to see.
Napping at work **SKILL:** *Identifying persuasive techniques*	Habits you want to change **SKILL:** *Using rhetorical questions*	Houseboats Pillows	...ask open questions. ...use context clues. ...use rhetorical questions.
Life of a King **SKILL:** *Identifying points of view*	Describing a movie **SKILL:** *Using pictures to explain*	Cellphone romances Books	...ask myself questions about stories. ...use reported speech. ...identify points of view.
Junior detective **SKILL:** *Noticing repeated words*	An interesting news story **SKILL:** *Using an anchor image*	Lateness Service dogs	...explain my reasons. ...identify cause and effect in a reading. ...use an anchor image in a presentation.
Hotel troubles **SKILL:** *Using subtitles*	The best or worst trip **SKILL:** *Using superlatives for emphasis*	Popular travel destinations Vacation destinations	...listen for key words in travel stories. ...use the present perfect for experiences. ...use subtitles to understand a video.

WORD LIST PAGE 107   **AUDIO AND VIDEO SCRIPTS** PAGES 111–113

7 Leisure time

Vocabulary and Listening
Predicting content

Speaking
Adding information

Grammar
Present perfect and continuous

Reading and Writing
Scanning

Viewing
Identifying purpose

Presenting
Introducing a topic with images

1 VOCABULARY AND LISTENING

A Listen and repeat.
CD 2-01

1. go horseback riding

2. catch up with friends

3. practice martial arts

4. build a website

5. go to concerts

6. go to flea markets

7. do gardening

8. have brunch

B Complete the sentences.

1. Let's _____ this weekend for some live music.
2. John needs to _____ every day so he can get a black belt.
3. Cafes are good places to _____ you haven't seen in a long time.
4. Jenna can show you how to _____ on her computer.
5. I like to _____ and look for bargains.

C Listen to people talking about leisure activities. Write **T** (True) or **F** (False).
CD 2-02

___ 1. Both speakers listen to music in the park.
___ 2. The man started riding horses recently.
___ 3. The woman is 15 years old.
___ 4. The woman finished her site last month.

D **Listen Again** Circle the best answer that continues each conversation.
CD 2-02

1. a. Yeah, I'd love to. b. Thank you.
2. a. I've had three. b. Since I was 15.
3. a. I've had four. b. For eight years.
4. a. No, not yet. b. I've done it once.

LISTENING
Predicting content
Predict content by guessing what speakers will talk about. This helps you to pay attention to what you hear.

ONLINE PRACTICE

▶ **I can...** predict content about leisure time. ☐ Very well ☐ Well ☐ Not very well

42

2 SPEAKING

A Complete the sentences. Use the words below.

| practicing | doing | been | taking |

A: How have you _____ doing?
B: Just fine. What have you been _____?
A: Well, I've been _____ martial arts.
B: Really? Have you been _____ lessons?
A: Yes, at the college.

B Listen to the conversation. Then practice with a partner.

**SPEAKING
Adding information**
After you answer a question, add more information. This helps to continue and open up the conversation.

ONLINE PRACTICE

Tom: Hi, Kristin.
Kristin: Oh, hi, Tom. How have you been?
Tom: Just fine. How about you? Are you doing anything interesting?
Kristin: Well, just going horseback riding.
Tom: I didn't know that. Have you been taking lessons?
Kristin: Yes, at BTA Stables. I've already taken eight lessons.
Tom: No kidding. How are you doing?
Kristin: Pretty well. I think I'm becoming a really good rider.

C **Pronunciation** **Reductions of *have*** Listen and repeat. People often reduce *have* in *Wh-* questions.

1. What have you been doing?
2. What have you been learning?
3. How many have you had?
4. How long have you worked here?

CULTURE TALK!

More people get hurt from horseback riding than riding motorcycles in the U.S. Which activity do you think is more dangerous?

D Work in pairs. Practice the conversation below. Add information.

A: I haven't seen you for a while. What have you been doing?
B: Just _____.
A: How are you doing?
B: Great! I think _____.

I can... add information to continue a conversation.   ☐ Very well   ☐ Well   ☐ Not very well

UNIT 7   43

3 GRAMMAR

A Listen. Then listen again and repeat.

Grammar Reference page 88

Present perfect continuous	Present perfect
What **have** you **been doing** lately? I**'ve been building** websites.	How many websites **have** you **built**? I**'ve built** three sites.
What **has** he **been doing** lately? He**'s been going** to concerts.	How many concerts **has** he **gone** to? He**'s gone** to three concerts this week.
What **have** they **been doing** lately? They**'ve been playing** pickleball.	How many games **have** they **played**? They**'ve played** four games.

NOTES:
- Use the present perfect to talk about things that are completed.
- Use the present perfect continuous to talk about continuing situations.

B Complete the conversation using the present perfect continuous or the present perfect and the words in parentheses.

A: ¹_____ you in a long time. (I / not / see)

B: I know. What ²_____ lately? (you / do)

A: Oh, not much really. ³_____ up with my friends a lot lately. (I / catch)

B: Me, too. ⁴_____ all my time with Jake and Susie at the café. (I / spend)

A: Yeah. ⁵_____ to the café three times already this week. (I / go)

C Work in pairs. Ask and answer questions. Use the present perfect or the present perfect continuous.

Example:
you

A: What have you been doing lately?
B: I've been gardening.

Example:
Jennifer / three today

A: How many jobs has Jennifer applied for today?
B: She's applied for three jobs today.

1. Rachel / four websites this week

2. Marco

3. you and your friends

4. Liz

5. you / three times this week

6. Rob

D Grammar Talk! How many times has Rosa...? Student A page 100, Student B page 103.

 I can... use the present perfect and its continuous tense.   ☐ Very well   ☐ Well   ☐ Not very well

4 READING AND WRITING

A Scan the text quickly. Answer the questions below.

1. How many people posted information on the site?
2. Who went to a concert?

> **READING**
> **Scanning**
> Scanning is looking quickly at a passage to find specific information. For example, look for names and numbers.

ONLINE PRACTICE

Profile
Photos (51)
Notes
Friends

Melanie Chin APRIL 27

Art and I just came back from a day-long horseback riding trip in Borrego Springs. We've been taking horseback riding lessons since January. We saw fantastic wild flowers that were in full bloom. What about you?

Mario Perez APRIL 30

What a week. I went to a concert at Oxford Hall and saw Girls' Generation. They were fantastic and they had great stage presence. And I've been getting a lot of exercise. I've played tennis with Mark three times this week. I won every game. I've also been practicing martial arts at the Planet Dojo school.

Sachi Nakamura MAY 1

This week, I've been building a website for a new pet store. Check it out here: PetPlace. When I haven't been building websites, I've been hanging out a lot with some old pals.

Danny Smith MAY 1

All I've been doing this week is studying. I haven't watched TV, so you know how busy I've been. I really need to get some shut-eye.

 B Read and listen. Then answer the following questions about the website.
CD 2–06

1. Who did Melanie go horseback riding with?
2. What did Mario do this week?
3. What do you think Sachi's job is?
4. What has Danny **not** been doing?

C Take notes in the chart. Write a paragraph about what you've been doing lately.

I've been...	How many times?	Where have you been doing this?

I can... scan information in a text. ☐ Very well ☐ Well ☐ Not very well

5 VIEWING: Chinese opera star

A Look at the photo of these opera singers. Discuss the questions below with a partner.

1. Do you like opera music? Why or why not?
2. What do you know about Chinese opera? Have you ever been to one?

B Watch the video. Circle the purpose of the video. There may be more than one correct answer.

a. To share the Chinese culture
b. To inform viewers about an interesting person
c. To encourage young people to join the orchestra
d. To advertise Tyler's school
e. To teach people how to sing in Chinese

> **VIEWING**
> **Identifying purpose**
> Think about the purpose and reason behind the video. Ask yourself *Why did someone make this?* or *What does the video do?*
>
> ONLINE PRACTICE

C Watch again. Read the statements. Write **T** (true) or **F** (false).

___ 1. Tyler speaks Chinese very well.
___ 2. Several people in Tyler's family also sing.
___ 3. Sherlyn Chew teaches children to speak Chinese.
___ 4. Tyler only sings by himself.
___ 5. All of the audience members are Chinese.
___ 6. Tyler has helped to bring Chinese and American cultures together.

D Work with a partner. Write an imaginary interview with Tyler. Ask and answer at least five questions. Use the model to help you.

A: So, Tyler. How do you like singing in a Chinese opera?
B: Well, I think it's…

I can… identify purpose in a video. ☐ Very well ☐ Well ☐ Not very well

6 PRESENTING

A Look at the photos about a person's leisure activity. What do you think the activity is?

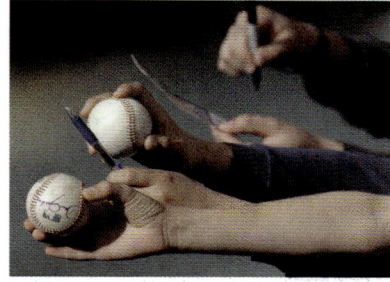

PRESENTING
Introducing a topic with images
Use interesting images to introduce your presentation. They make your presentation more exciting, and they help people remember it.

ONLINE PRACTICE

B Listen to the presentation. Was your guess in Part A correct?
CD 2-07

C Do you know someone who does an interesting activity? Make notes in the chart. Find memorable pictures that show the activity.

Activity	How long	Other details

CULTURE TALK!

Collecting autographs is a $50-million-a-year industry, especially in places like Los Angeles. Do you think this is a real job or just a hobby?

D Stand up. Show a group your photos. Then use your notes from Part C to present about the activity.
PRESENT

TIP

Encourage your audience to guess about your pictures before you tell them.

 I can... introduce a topic with images. ☐ Very well ☐ Well ☐ Not very well

47

8 Appearance

Vocabulary and Listening
Listening for descriptive words

Speaking
Using phrases to agree

Grammar
Used to

Reading and Writing
Making a cluster diagram

Viewing
Making predictions

Presenting
Focusing on key points

1 VOCABULARY AND LISTENING

CD 2-08

A Listen and repeat.

1. mustache

2. wavy hair

3. bald

4. beard

5. scruffy

6. neat

7. confident

8. studious

B Write the correct words from Part A next to their opposites below.

ONLINE PRACTICE

1. lazy _____
2. hairy _____
3. shy _____
4. straight hair _____
5. neat _____

C Listen to people talking. Cross out the word that does **not** describe the people.

CD 2-09

1. bald   confident   mustache
2. beard   neat   scruffy
3. messy   neat   studious
4. scruffy   confident   organized

> **LISTENING**
> **Listening for descriptive words**
> To identify people, listen for descriptive words such as adjectives and nouns that the adjectives describe.
>
> ONLINE PRACTICE

D Write **T** (True) or **F** (False).

CD 2-09

____ 1. The new manager works in the cafeteria.
____ 2. Jay has a mustache.
____ 3. People say that Allison is studious.
____ 4. Both speakers are probably on vacation.

> **I can...** listen for descriptive words about appearance. ☐ Very well ☐ Well ☐ Not very well

48

2 SPEAKING

A Match the questions and answers.

Speaker A
___ 1. Who is that over there?
___ 2. Mark? Why does he look so different?
___ 3. You're right. What else is different?

Speaker B
a. It's his mustache.
b. His hair is shorter, too.
c. That's Mark Gomez.

B Listen to the conversation. Then practice with a partner.
CD 2-10

Spira: Is that Kim Fisher? She looks so different.
Sophie: That's true. She used to have really long hair. Look how short it is now. Doesn't she look great?
Spira: You're right, she does. Remember how she used to be kind of scruffy? How did she get to be so neat?
Sophie: I don't know, but she really has changed a lot. By the way, so have you. You didn't used to look so confident.
Spira: I know. I used to be shy when I was younger.

> **SPEAKING**
> **Using phrases to agree**
> Use expressions such as *I know*, *That's true*, and *You're right* to show that you agree with what the speaker said.
>
> ONLINE PRACTICE

C Work in pairs. Practice the conversation below by describing a student in the classroom. Use expressions to agree.

A: This student _____.
B: Oh, is it _____?
A: Yes. Doesn't he/she look _____?
B: You're right.

 **D** Pronunciation Consonant clusters with s Listen and repeat.
CD 2-11 Notice the sound of *s* with other sounds.

1. **s**cruffy
2. **s**chool
3. **s**tudious
4. **s**traight

 **I can...** use phrases to agree.   ☐ Very well   ☐ Well   ☐ Not very well

3 GRAMMAR

A Listen. Then listen again and repeat.

Grammar Reference page 89

Used to	
Did you **use to be** neat?	Yes, I **did**. I **used to be** neat.
Did he **use to have** a mustache?	No, he **didn't**. He **used to have** a beard.
How **did** you **use to go** to school?	We **used to** walk, but now we drive.

NOTES:
- *Used to* is for things that were true in the past but are no longer true in the present.
- *Used to* is for affirmative statements, and *use to* for questions and negative statements.

B Complete the sentences with *used to* and the verbs in parentheses.

1. Did you _____ to school? (walk)
2. I _____ the subway to school. (not / take)
3. Gemma _____ her skateboard to school. (ride)
4. Larry _____ so lazy. (not / be)
5. I _____ scruffy, but now I'm much neater. (look)

C Work in pairs. Ask and answer questions with *used to*.

Example:

Mark / have a beard

A: Did Mark use to have a beard?

B: No, he didn't. He used to have a mustache.

1. Ana / have long hair

2. Jeremy / be scruffy

3. Claudia and Tim / be neat

4. Abby / have straight hair

5. Emma / be confident

6. you / walk to school

D Grammar Talk! **Did she use to…?** Student A page 100, Student B page 103.

I can… ask and answer questions with *used to*. ☐ Very well   ☐ Well   ☐ Not very well

50

4 READING AND WRITING

A Read and listen. Why do some people choose not to go to reunions anymore?
CD 2-13

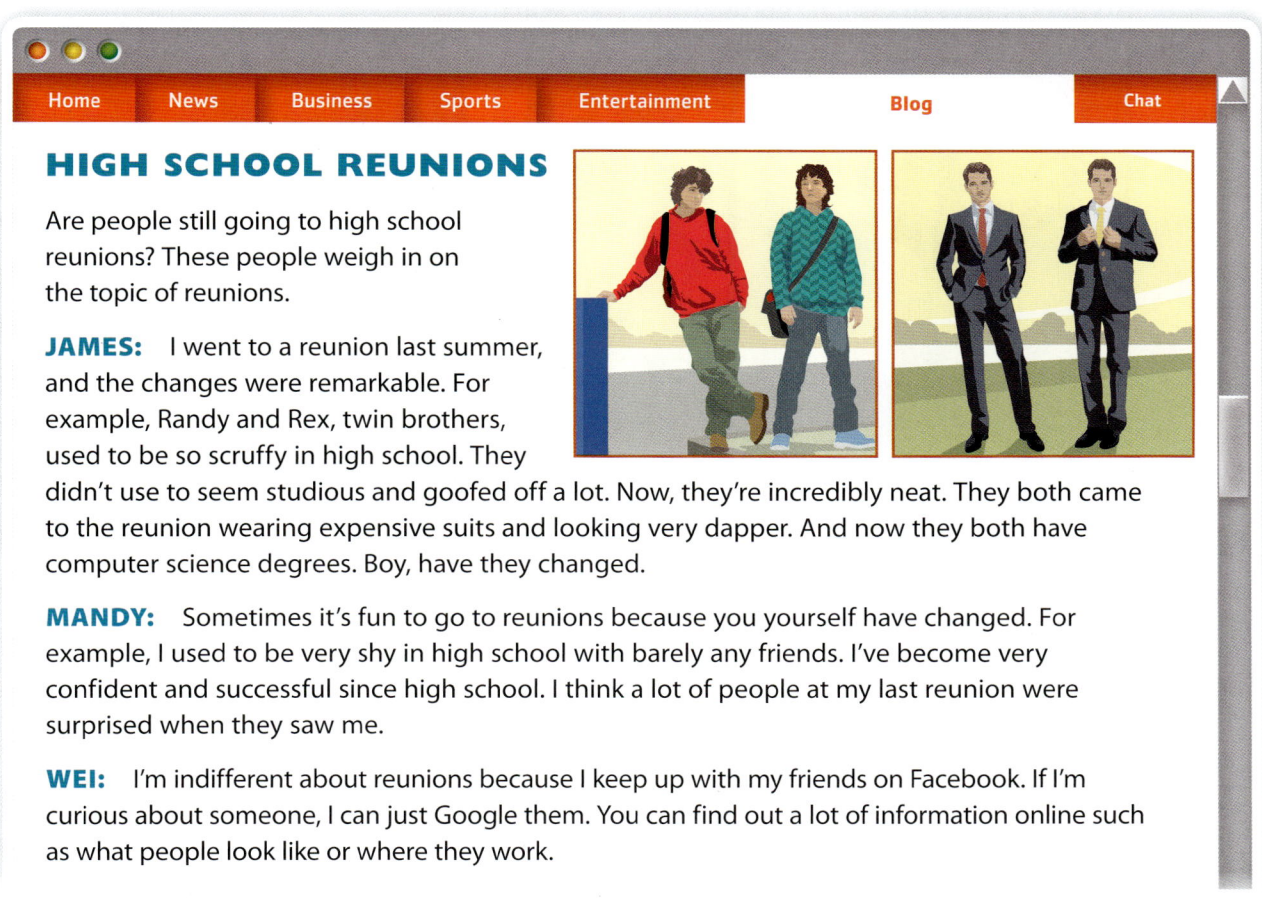

HIGH SCHOOL REUNIONS

Are people still going to high school reunions? These people weigh in on the topic of reunions.

JAMES: I went to a reunion last summer, and the changes were remarkable. For example, Randy and Rex, twin brothers, used to be so scruffy in high school. They didn't use to seem studious and goofed off a lot. Now, they're incredibly neat. They both came to the reunion wearing expensive suits and looking very dapper. And now they both have computer science degrees. Boy, have they changed.

MANDY: Sometimes it's fun to go to reunions because you yourself have changed. For example, I used to be very shy in high school with barely any friends. I've become very confident and successful since high school. I think a lot of people at my last reunion were surprised when they saw me.

WEI: I'm indifferent about reunions because I keep up with my friends on Facebook. If I'm curious about someone, I can just Google them. You can find out a lot of information online such as what people look like or where they work.

B Read the statements about the blog. Write **T** (True) or **F** (False).

___ 1. Rex and Randy are friends. ___ 3. Mandy was confident in high school.
___ 2. Rex and Randy went to college. ___ 4. Wei likes to go to reunions.

C Describe someone who has changed. Give examples. Use the cluster diagram to take notes.

[Cluster diagram with central box, branching to "Personality" and "Appearance"]

> **WRITING**
> **Making a cluster diagram**
> A cluster diagram helps you brainstorm. Write down your main idea, along with supporting ideas and examples.
>
> ONLINE PRACTICE

Before: _____ Before: _____
After: _____ After: _____

D Write a paragraph about how a person has changed. Use your notes from Part C.

I can... make a cluster diagram before writing.   ☐ Very well   ☐ Well   ☐ Not very well

UNIT 8 **51**

5 VIEWING: Stuart's new look

A Look at the photos. Lisa and Mica are going to give Stuart a makeover. What changes to his look do you think they will make?

Mica   Lisa

B Watch the video. Did Stuart's makeover include any of the changes you predicted in Part A?

C Watch again. Complete the chart about Stuart.

	Before	After
Hair		
Clothes		
Personality		

VIEWING
Making predictions
Before you watch, predict what you think is going to happen in the video. This helps you focus on the content.

ONLINE PRACTICE

D Think of a famous person. What changes would you make? Complete the chart. Then discuss your ideas with a partner.

Famous Person: _____

	Before	After
Hair		
Clothes		
Personality		

CULTURE TALK!

Makeover TV shows are popular in Brazil. Are they popular in your country? Do you like to watch them?

> **I can...** make predictions about what I'm going to see.   ☐ Very well   ☐ Well   ☐ Not very well

52

6 PRESENTING

A Read the presentation. Underline and number the four key points.

> **PRESENTING**
> **Focusing on key points**
> Focus on 3–5 key points. If you make too many points, it will be difficult for your audience to remember them.
>
> ONLINE PRACTICE

"I've changed a lot since high school. First, my hair is very different. I used to have short, curly hair, but now my hair is straight and a little longer. I used to be short, but now I'm pretty tall. My personality has changed, too. In high school I was shy and studious, but now I'm a lot more confident and outgoing. And I'm more relaxed… I don't work as hard as I used to."

B Close your book. Try to list the key points in the presentation. Can you remember them all?

C Think of a time in your past. How have you changed since then? Make notes in the chart. Try to find a photo of yourself at that time.

Before	Now

D Stand up. Use your notes from Part C to tell your classmates how you have changed. At the end of your presentation, show them an old photo of yourself.

PRESENT

CULTURE TALK!
High school reunions are becoming less popular in the U.S. Are they popular in your country? Would you like to go to one?

TIP
Use hand gestures to describe appearance — for example, your hair or height.

I can... focus on key points. ☐ Very well ☐ Well ☐ Not very well

53

9 Habits

Vocabulary and Listening
Listening for frequency words

Speaking
Asking open questions

Grammar
Questions with *How long*

Reading and Writing
Using context clues

Viewing
Identifying persuasive techniques

Presenting
Using rhetorical questions

1 VOCABULARY AND LISTENING

A Listen and repeat.
CD 2-14

1. get up early

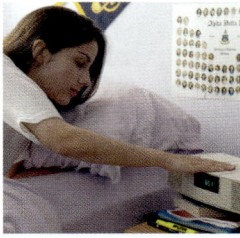
2. use an alarm

3. do chores

4. ride a bike to school

5. go to bed late

6. check my messages

7. catch up on the news

8. take out the trash

B Complete the sentences with the correct words from Part A.

ONLINE PRACTICE

I spend long hours at work, and I have to keep my phone off during the day. So as soon as I get home, I ¹_____. After dinner, I ²_____ on TV because I always want to know what's happening in the world. When I go to bed, I have to ³_____ or I won't wake up on time. Sometimes I ⁴_____, but then I'm tired the next morning.

C Listen to people talking about everyday habits. Number the habits from *1–4*.
CD 2-15

___ doing chores   ___ going to bed late
___ riding a bike   ___ getting up early

D **Listen Again** Check ✓ how often each person does the habit.
CD 2-15

1. ☐ almost always   ☐ hardly ever
2. ☐ never   ☐ every day
3. ☐ almost every day   ☐ once in a while
4. ☐ every Sunday   ☐ every afternoon

> **LISTENING**
> **Listening for frequency words**
> To answer questions with *How often?*, listen for frequency words such as *always*, *often*, and *never*.
>
> ONLINE PRACTICE

I can... listen for frequency words about habits. ☐ Very well ☐ Well ☐ Not very well

54

2 SPEAKING

A Put the conversation in order. Number the sentences *1–6*.

___ I studied it in Taipei.
___ How long were you there?
___ I loved it. The food is great.
___ Two years! How did you like it there?
___ So tell me. Where did you study Chinese?
___ I was there for two years.

B Listen to the conversation. Then practice with a partner.
CD 2-16

Jade: Welcome to the Jade Jackson show. Today, I'm talking to the handsome actor, Stone Smith. Stone, could you tell me about your early life?

Stone: Well, when I was little, I used to get up early and ride my horse to school every day.

Jade: Where did you grow up?

Stone: I grew up in Texas. Not far from Houston.

Jade: I see. And how long have you wanted to be an actor?

Stone: Oh, I've wanted to be an actor since I was a kid. After high school, I moved to New York to study acting.

Jade: Where did you study acting?

Stone: At the Acting Studio. After that, I got my first acting job on TV.

SPEAKING
Asking open questions

Begin questions with *Tell me about...* to ask open questions and to get the speakers to give you more information.

ONLINE PRACTICE

C Work in pairs. Practice the conversation below with your own information. Ask open questions.

A: Could you tell me something about your early life?
B: Well, when I was little, I _____.
A: Where _____?
B: I _____.
A: How long _____?

D **Pronunciation** **Past tense endings** Listen and repeat. Regular verbs have three different sounds in the past.
CD 2-17

checked / worked   moved / lived   wanted / waited

I can... ask open questions. ☐ Very well ☐ Well ☐ Not very well

UNIT 9   55

3 GRAMMAR

 A Listen. Then listen again and repeat.

Grammar Reference page 90

Simple past, present perfect, and present perfect continuous with *How long*	
How long were you a teacher? **How long did** you **live** in Osaka?	I **was** a teacher from 2005 to 2012. I **lived** there for ten years.
How long have you **been** a photographer? **How long have** you **studied** Chinese?	I**'ve been** a photographer for five years. I**'ve studied** Chinese for six months.
How long have you **been** living here?	I**'ve been living** here since 2010.

NOTES:
- Use *how long* with the simple past to ask about situations that have ended.
- Use *how long* with the present perfect or present perfect continuous to ask about situations or actions that are continuing.

B Complete the interview questions with *how long* and the correct form of the verbs.

A: So tell me. ¹_____ you _____ in Los Angeles? (live)

B: I've lived here since 2006.

A: And ²_____ you _____ as a musician? (work)

B: I've been working as a musician for ten years.

A: ³_____ you _____ to be a musician? (want)

B: I have wanted to be a musician since I was in high school.

A: ⁴_____ you in a band? (be)

B: I was in a band for four years.

A: ⁵_____ you _____ music lessons? (take)

B: I took music lessons for ten years.

C Work in pairs. Ask and answer questions. Use the correct tense.

Example: you / since I was 10

A: How long have you been doing chores?   B: I've been doing chores since I was 10.

1. he / for two years

2. Mark and Erik / San Francisco / for 5 years

3. Robbie / since last year

4. Maria / since last month

5. Ed / since he got a job

6. Matt / for a few minutes

D *Grammar Talk!* How long has she been...? Student A page 101, Student B page 104.

 I can... ask questions with *How long*. ☐ Very well ☐ Well ☐ Not very well

56

4 READING AND WRITING

A Read and listen. What kind of home does Rob Santos have?

At Home on the Water

Ever wonder what it might be like to live on a boat year-round? It sounded fascinating to me, so I decided to interview Rob Santos, who lives on a houseboat in Sausalito.

Tell me, Rob, how long have you been living on your boat?

I was living in an apartment in San Francisco, and I was driving over here to work at Zotz Studios one day. I'm an animator, and I had just finished working on a cartoon about boats. I always wanted to live in Sausalito and be near my job. I was looking for a house, but they're so expensive! I found an old houseboat that needed a lot of repair—a real fixer-upper—for about half of what a house usually costs in Sausalito.

How long have these houseboats been here?

Well, they used to build ships here. When the shipbuilding stopped, there were a lot of leftover materials—pieces of wood, glass, and metal. Some bohemian kids moved here. They wanted a free lifestyle—they didn't have any money, and they didn't want regular jobs. They lived cheaply by building many of these houseboats out of the junk they found lying around.

How fascinating! So tell me something about your daily life.

I sleep great. The boat rocks gently all night. I ride my bike to work, and it only takes about ten minutes. It's a nice life.

> **READING**
> **Using context clues**
> Context clues—phrases around unknown words—often help you guess and understand the meanings of unknown words.
>
> ONLINE PRACTICE

B Find and circle in the interview the bold words below. Underline their context clues. Then answer the questions.

1. As an **animator**, what kind of work does Rob do?
2. Why might a **fixer-upper** be less expensive than a regular house?
3. What kind of **materials** are many of the Sausalito houseboats made from?
4. Why might junk that is lying around be useful for **bohemians**?

C Interview and ask a classmate questions about their life or job. Write down notes on a separate piece of paper.

D Use your notes and write a paragraph about your classmate's life. Use information from your chart.

> **CULTURE TALK!**
>
> About 15,000 people live on houseboats in the United Kingdom. Would you like to live on a boat? Why or why not?

I can... use context clues.   ☐ Very well   ☐ Well   ☐ Not very well

UNIT 9

5 VIEWING: Napping at work

A Look at the photos. What do you think these people are doing?

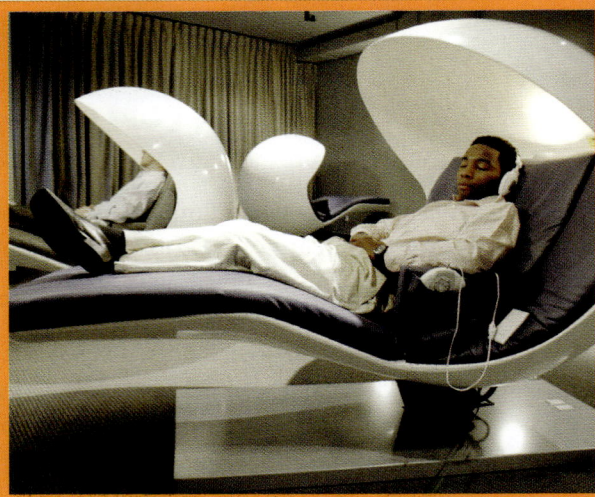

B Watch the video. Which persuasive techniques does it use? Check ✓ them.
1. Regular people like you are doing it.
2. It's a great price, so buy it now!
3. Science proves that it works.
4. Famous people use it, too.
5. It's better than another company's product.

> **VIEWING**
> **Identifying persuasive techniques**
> Advertisers use different techniques to get people to buy their product. Try to identify them as you watch.
>
> ONLINE PRACTICE

C Watch again. Complete the sentences.
1. Just because you're _____ all day does not mean that you're going to be productive.
2. Because workers can take _____ breaks, they should take sleeping breaks, too.
3. More than _____ percent of 24-hour companies let workers sleep.
4. We all _____ down at various points during the day.
5. Science shows that having a nap can revive a _____ mind.
6. Jo has more _____ after napping.

D Work with a partner. Ask and answer the questions in the sleep survey.
1. How many hours do you usually sleep at night?
2. Do you ever nap? How often? For how long?
3. Do you usually get enough sleep?
4. How do you feel when you don't get enough sleep?
5. Do you think napping at work is a good idea? Why or why not?

> **CULTURE TALK!**
>
> In Mexico, 30% of people sleep with two pillows. How many pillows do you use when you sleep?

I can... identify persuasive techniques. ☐ Very well ☐ Well ☐ Not very well

6 PRESENTING

A Read the presentation. What three habits does the speaker want to change?

**PRESENTING
Using rhetorical questions**
Use rhetorical questions (questions we don't expect people to answer) to get the attention of your audience.

ONLINE PRACTICE

" Do you waste a lot of time on the Internet every day? I do. I spend hours on social networking sites, watching silly videos, and gaming. I should really spend less time online. Then I'd have more time for more important things, like seeing friends, studying, and exercising.

_____? So do I. I know I should go to bed around ten so I can get enough sleep, but I usually stay up past midnight. I think I'm going to try to go to bed an hour earlier every night. Then I'll have more energy during the day.

_____? Then you're like me. I should eat healthy snacks, but I prefer junk food like potato chips and candy. I'd really like to have a healthier diet, but that's hard to do. "

B Read the presentation again. Underline the rhetorical question. Then write two more rhetorical questions in the blanks.

C Think of three habits you want to change. Make notes in the chart.

Habit	Why I want to change the habit
1.	
2.	
3.	

TIP

Ask rhetorical questions so your audience members can agree with you.

D Stand up. Use your notes from Part C to tell a group about habits you'd like to change. Use rhetorical questions.

PRESENT

 **I can...** use rhetorical questions. ☐ Very well ☐ Well ☐ Not very well

59

Self-Assessment

1 VOCABULARY

Circle the correct word or words to complete each sentence.

1. I like to *build websites* / *have brunch* / *catch up with friends* on the weekends and see how they're doing.
2. I *do gardening* / *go to flea markets* / *go horseback riding* to relax. I grow vegetables and flowers in my backyard.
3. I love live music, so I *practice martial arts* / *go to flea markets* / *go to concerts*.

I can... understand vocabulary about leisure time. (Unit 7)

4. Jason doesn't have any hair on his head. He's *neat* / *bald* / *scruffy*.
5. Mike's chin itches because he is growing *a beard* / *a mustache* / *wavy hair*.
6. Ken's shirt is wrinkled, he hasn't shaved, and his hair is messy. He looks *studious* / *confident* / *scruffy*.

I can... understand vocabulary about appearance. (Unit 8)

7. I don't like to *get up early* / *go to bed late* / *do chores*. I'm usually in a bad mood in the morning.
8. Karen doesn't drive to school. She *uses an alarm* / *does chores* / *rides her bike*.
9. I called you this morning. Did you *catch up on the news* / *take out the trash* / *check your messages*?
10. I don't have to *use an alarm* / *go to bed late* / *get up early*. My roommate wakes me up.

I can... understand vocabulary about habits. (Unit 9)

2 GRAMMAR

1. We *haven't visiting* / *haven't visited* / *haven't been visiting* my parents in over a year.
2. What *have you been* / *you been doing* / *have you been doing* lately?
3. Kara *has gone* / *has been going* / *have been going* to Mexico five times.

I can... use the present perfect and the present perfect continuous. (Unit 7)

4. I *used to have* / *use to have* / *use to had* a beard.
5. Did he *used to look* / *use to looked* / *use to look* neat?
6. Mark didn't *used to be* / *use to was* / *use to be* scruffy.

I can... ask and answer questions with *used to*. (Unit 8)

7. How long *have you live* / *did you live* / *have you living* in Texas?
8. How long *did she took* / *she has taken* / *has she been taking* piano lessons?
9. How long *have you stayed* / *have you been staying* / *did you stay* at Robert's house last night?
10. We have *been waiting* / *wait* / *waiting* for about thirty minutes and the food is still not here.

I can... ask questions with *How long*. (Unit 9)

Units 7-9

3 READING

A Read and listen to the blog post. What event did the writer go to?

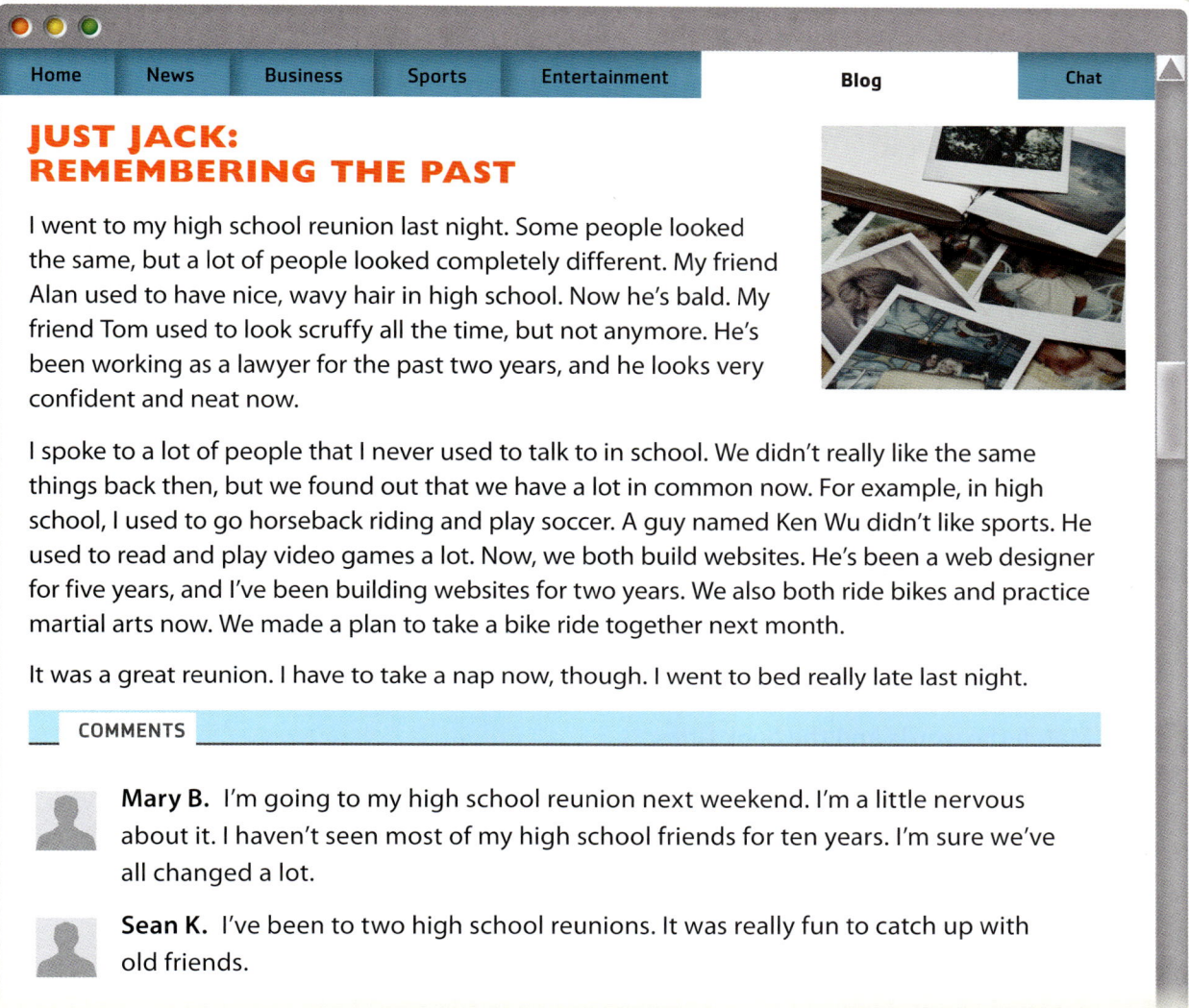

JUST JACK: REMEMBERING THE PAST

I went to my high school reunion last night. Some people looked the same, but a lot of people looked completely different. My friend Alan used to have nice, wavy hair in high school. Now he's bald. My friend Tom used to look scruffy all the time, but not anymore. He's been working as a lawyer for the past two years, and he looks very confident and neat now.

I spoke to a lot of people that I never used to talk to in school. We didn't really like the same things back then, but we found out that we have a lot in common now. For example, in high school, I used to go horseback riding and play soccer. A guy named Ken Wu didn't like sports. He used to read and play video games a lot. Now, we both build websites. He's been a web designer for five years, and I've been building websites for two years. We also both ride bikes and practice martial arts now. We made a plan to take a bike ride together next month.

It was a great reunion. I have to take a nap now, though. I went to bed really late last night.

COMMENTS

Mary B. I'm going to my high school reunion next weekend. I'm a little nervous about it. I haven't seen most of my high school friends for ten years. I'm sure we've all changed a lot.

Sean K. I've been to two high school reunions. It was really fun to catch up with old friends.

B Answer each question with information from the blog post.
1. What did Jack's friend Alan use to look like?
2. What has Jack's friend Tom been doing?
3. How long has Ken Wu been building websites?
4. When will Mary see her high school friends?
5. How many reunions has Sean been to?

C Imagine that you are at your ten-year school reunion. Describe what people were like in school and what they're like now.

10 Stories

Vocabulary and Listening
Asking yourself questions
Speaking
Refusing politely
Grammar
Reported speech
Reading and Writing
Summarizing
Viewing
Identifying points of view
Presenting
Using pictures to explain

1 VOCABULARY AND LISTENING

 A Listen and repeat.
CD 2-21

1. mystery 2. science fiction 3. western 4. biography

5. romance 6. fantasy 7. historical fiction 8. children's literature

B Match the words and the book titles.

____ 1. western   a. *Space Adventure 2053*
____ 2. science fiction b. *Paul Cezanne: A Great Painter*
____ 3. romance   c. *A Cowboy's Story*
____ 4. biography   d. *Our Hearts Together Forever*

C You are going to listen to parts of each book below. Write one
CD 2-22 question about the books. Listen and answer your question. Then number the books from *1–4*.

Your question _____ ?

____ *Space Adventure 2053*   ____ *Our Hearts Together Forever*
____ *A Cowboy's Story*   ____ *Paul Cezanne: A Great Painter*

LISTENING
Asking yourself questions
When you know the topic, ask yourself questions about it before you listen. This helps you prepare to listen.

ONLINE PRACTICE

D Listen Again Write **T** (True) or **F** (False).
CD 2-22
____ 1. Paul Cezanne studied to become a lawyer.
____ 2. The man came from Silver Rush.
____ 3. The man wants to marry the woman.
____ 4. The story takes place in the future.

 I can... ask myself questions about stories.   ☐ Very well   ☐ Well   ☐ Not very well

2 SPEAKING

A Complete the sentences with the words below.

| called | done | movie | reading | thanks | which |

A: Hey, do you want to go to a _____?
B: Sorry, I'm busy. I'm _____ this great book.
A: _____ one?
B: A mystery _____ *The Man Who Came Back*. You can have it when I'm _____.
A: _____!

B Listen to the conversation. Then practice with a partner.

Ben: Hi, Jill. It's Ben.
Jill: Oh, hi, Ben. Say, have you written your paper for history class yet?
Ben: Not yet, but are you free tonight? I'd like to go over my notes with you.
Jill: Sorry, but I'm busy. I have to work on an essay on science fiction novels for my English class.
Ben: That's right. You told me you were doing that. Well, maybe we can work on the history paper next week.
Jill: Sure. Sounds good.

> **SPEAKING**
> **Refusing politely**
> Use *Sorry, but...* with an explanation to refuse a request politely. Use *Maybe we can...* to offer an alternative or a different option.
>
> ONLINE PRACTICE

C Work in pairs. Practice the conversation below with your own information. Refuse politely and offer an alternative.

A: Are you free tonight? I'd like to _____.
B: Sorry, I'm busy. I have to _____.
A: Oh, that's right.
B: Maybe we can _____ next week.

D **Pronunciation** **Plural nouns.** Listen and repeat. Nouns have three sounds in the plural form.

1. notes / books
2. westerns / biographies
3. classes / romances

> **I can...** use expressions to refuse politely. ☐ Very well ☐ Well ☐ Not very well

UNIT 10 63

3 GRAMMAR

A Listen. Then listen again and repeat.

Grammar Reference page 91

Reported speech	
Direct statements and questions	**Reported statements and questions**
"I'm tired of ghost stories," he said.	He **said / told me** he **was** tired of ghost stories.
"Sam **read** Einstein's biography," he said.	He **said / told me** Sam **had read** Einstein's biography.
"I've seen that western," he said.	He **said / told me** he **had seen** that western.
"**Are** you **reading** a biography?" she asked.	She **asked me** if I **was reading** a biography.

B Complete the reported sentences with the correct form of the verb.

1. "I'm late," she said. → She said she _____.
2. "We're leaving," they said. → They told us they _____.
3. "I have to write an essay," she said. → She told us she _____.
4. "I saw the new mystery," he said. → He said he _____.
5. "They've left," she said. → She said they _____.

C Work in pairs. Report what the people said.

Example:

I'm at the bookstore now.

A: What did she say?

B: She said she was at the bookstore.

1. I read yesterday's newspaper.

2. I told my friends a funny story.

3. We have seen that movie.

4. I'm walking my dogs.

5. I'm having car problems.

6. Is the store open today?

D **Grammar Talk!** Do you like…? Student A page 101, Student B page 104.

I can… use reported speech.   ☐ Very well   ☐ Well   ☐ Not very well

64

4 READING AND WRITING

A Read and listen. How many paragraphs are there in the book review below?

BOOK REVIEWS

The Voyages of Zheng He

I love an exciting adventure story, and when I learn fascinating facts and a bit of history at the same time, so much the better. This is exactly what you get with *The Voyages of Zheng He*, the new work of historical fiction by Victor Guzman.

Here's the story: Zheng He was a Chinese explorer who led expeditions throughout Asia, the Middle East, and Africa in the early part of the 15th century. Working with the emperor Zhu Di, and leading his army, Zheng He commanded a fleet of 317 ships and 28,000 crewmen. Zheng He went on seven expeditions all together, in order to increase China's trade and knowledge of the world.

The Voyages of Zheng He is a work of fiction, but Guzman did a lot of research. He interviewed Chinese historians and also traveled to many of the places Zheng He visited. As a result, the story is full of realistic details about Zheng He's life and times. We learn all about the people and the places Zheng He encountered in his travels. *The Voyages of Zheng He* is an entertaining way to learn more about Chinese history. I highly recommend it.

B Answer the questions about the book review in Part A.
1. In which paragraph does the writer of the book review say what the book is about?
2. In which paragraph does the writer of the book review say her opinion of the book?
3. Why did Zheng He go on seven expeditions?
4. How did the author, Victor Guzman, do research for the book?
5. Why does the writer of the book review like this book?

C Think about a book you read. What was it about? What was your opinion? Write down notes on a separate piece of paper.

D Write a book review with a summary of the main events in one paragraph and your opinion in another paragraph. Use your notes in Part C.

CULTURE TALK!

Cellphone romances—romances written on and for cell phones—are popular in Japan. Do you read books on your phone? Why or why not?

WRITING
Summarizing
When you write a book review, you give a summary and explain the main events only. Leave out small details that aren't important.

ONLINE PRACTICE

I can... write a summary.   ☐ Very well   ☐ Well   ☐ Not very well

5 VIEWING: Life of a King

A Look at the photo. What do you know about Stephen King?

B Watch the video about Stephen King. Check ✓ the things it talks about.

- ☐ 1. family
- ☐ 2. fears
- ☐ 3. movies
- ☐ 4. free-time activities
- ☐ 5. critics' opinions of his books
- ☐ 6. plans for the future

C Watch again. Read the statements and identify the point of view. Write **S** (Stephen King), **T** (Tabitha, Stephen King's wife), **I** (Interviewer), or **C** (Critic).

____ 1. I'm afraid of the same things people are afraid of.
____ 2. I don't think his books and stories are too strange.
____ 3. His books make you feel like you know and understand the places and people.
____ 4. Stephen King likes to have fun.
____ 5. I have never read books by Jane Austen.
____ 6. Stephen King's books are badly written.

D Work with a partner. Answer the questions about a writer you like.

1. What kinds of books does he/she write?
2. Which books have you read? Which was your favorite?
3. Did the books become movies? If not, would the books make good movies?
4. What do you know about the writer's personal life?

VIEWING
Identifying points of view

As you watch a video, try to identify the different points of view for each person. Who expresses each opinion?

ONLINE PRACTICE

CULTURE TALK!

Thirty-two percent of Americans have read between one and five books in the past twelve months. How many books have you read recently?

I can... identify points of view.   ☐ Very well   ☐ Well   ☐ Not very well

66

6 PRESENTING

A Read the presentation and look at the picture. What does the picture tell you that the words do not?

PRESENTING
Using pictures to explain
Try to find good pictures for your presentation. You don't need to use as many words with good pictures.

ONLINE PRACTICE

> My favorite book and movie is *Life of Pi*. Most of the movie takes place on a small lifeboat in the middle of the ocean. The main character is a teenage boy named Pi. The other main character is a tiger named Richard Parker. They are on a ship on their way to Canada. There is a storm and the ship sinks, and Pi and several animals get into the boat. After the other animals die, Pi and the tiger spend more than seven months together on the boat. The book and the movie are both beautiful, and they really make you think about life.

B Cover the words in the presentation in Part A. Tell a partner about *Life of Pi*. Point to the picture as you are speaking.

C Think of a movie you liked. Find pictures from the movie. Make notes in the chart below.

Name of movie: _____

Main characters	Summary of main events	Why I liked it

TIP

Use the present tense to tell about a book or movie, even if it happened in the past.

PRESENT

D Stand up. Use your notes from Part C to tell a group about the movie. Point to the pictures as you speak.

I can... use pictures to explain a presentation. ☐ Very well ☐ Well ☐ Not very well

67

11 In the news

Vocabulary and Listening
Listening for main ideas

Speaking
Explaining your reasons

Grammar
While and *when* clauses

Reading and Writing
Identifying cause and effect (2)

Viewing
Noticing repeated words

Presenting
Using an anchor image

1 VOCABULARY AND LISTENING

 A Listen and repeat.
CD 2-27

1. flood   2. fire   3. crime   4. demonstration

5. election   6. sports event   7. fashion show   8. exhibition

B Complete the conversation with words from Part A.

A: Did you watch the news last night? I heard the _____ at the factory burned for three hours.

B: And did you see the part about the _____ in Grandview? Those houses were completely under water.

A: What a shame. But at least Rita Rodriguez won the _____ in Monrovia.

B: I heard! She can help the city stop _____.

A: Tell me about it. Anyway, let's go check out the _____ of Martin Yee's paintings at the museum.

 C Listen to the news reports. Number the events from *1–4*.
CD 2-28

____ a crime   ____ a fashion show

____ an exhibition   ____ a sports event

D **Listen Again** Write **T** (True) or **F** (False).
CD 2-28

____ 1. Over 800 people attended the event.
____ 2. The event in London happened this week.
____ 3. The event was held in Boston.
____ 4. The police suspect an employee.

> **LISTENING**
> **Listening for main ideas**
> Listen for main ideas in content words—nouns and verbs. You don't have to understand every word you hear.
>
> ONLINE PRACTICE

I can... understand main ideas.   ☐ Very well   ☐ Well   ☐ Not very well

2 SPEAKING

A Match the questions and answers.

Speaker A
___ 1. Where have you been?
___ 2. What happened?
___ 3. Are you OK?

Speaker B
a. Yes, I'm fine.
b. On the bus for the last hour.
c. The bus broke down.

B Listen to the conversation. Then practice with a partner.

> **SPEAKING**
> **Explaining your reasons**
> Apologize and give reasons when you are late. This makes the other person feel comfortable and puts them at ease.
>
> ONLINE PRACTICE

Max: Where have you been? I've been waiting for almost an hour.
Maria: **I'm sorry I'm late. I fell down and hurt my leg while I was running after a bus.**
Max: Oh, no. How's your leg now?
Maria: It hurts a little, but I think it's going to be OK.
Max: I was getting really worried about you. The news on TV said this storm is really bad.
Maria: I am really sorry for being so late.
Max: That's OK. You're here now. That's the important thing.

C Work in pairs. Practice the conversation below with your own information. Explain your reasons for being late.

A: Where have you been?
B: I'm sorry I'm late. I _____.
A: That's OK. You're here now. That's the important thing.

D **Pronunciation** *Let* vs. *late* Listen and repeat. Words like *let* and *late* are pronounced differently.

1. let / late
2. wet / wait
3. men / main
4. sell / sale

CULTURE TALK!

In Australia, it's rude to be late. Is this true in your country? Are you often late? What are some good reasons for being late?

I can... explain my reasons. ☐ Very well ☐ Well ☐ Not very well

UNIT 11 **69**

3 GRAMMAR

 A Listen. Then listen again and repeat.

Grammar Reference page 92

While clauses	When clauses
I saw an accident **while** I **was driving** to work.	I was driving to work **when** I **saw** an accident.
The earthquake hit **while** I **was sleeping**.	I was sleeping **when** the earthquake **hit**.

NOTES:
- Use *while* with the past progressive to describe an event in progress in the past.
- Use *when* with the simple past to describe a finished event in the past.

 B Use the cues to write sentences with *while* or *when*.

1. While the model _____ down the runway, photographers were busy taking pictures. (walk)
2. The criminal quickly ran away when he _____ the police cars coming. (see)
3. Soft background music was playing while people _____ the new exhibition. (view)
4. When the flood waters _____ rising, the father brought everyone up to the roof of the house. (start)
5. I was shocked when I _____ that the police arrested the movie star. (hear)

C Work in pairs. Ask and answer questions. Use *while* and *when* clauses.

Example:

Eun / the phone rang

A: What was Eun doing when the phone rang?
B: She was watching TV when the phone rang.

1. you / raining

2. Manuel / the news came on

3. Tracey and Lara / doing homework

4. Amy / sang

5. Adam / hurt his back

6. you / your friend visiting

D Grammar Talk! What was Manolo doing...? Student A page 102, Student B page 105.

I can... use *while* and *when* clauses. ☐ Very well ☐ Well ☐ Not very well

4 READING AND WRITING

A Read and listen. What is Ricochet's special skill?

Ricochet the SURFice™ Dog

Ricochet was trained to be a service dog to help disabled people, especially with tasks around the house. For example, Ricochet learned how to unzip a jacket and open a refrigerator door. She showed a lot of promise as a puppy—it looked like Ricochet was going to be a great service dog. But as she grew older, she became more interested in chasing birds than in doing her tasks. As a result, she had to leave the training program. However, Ricochet was smart—her owner saw how trainable she was, so she taught Ricochet how to surf. It didn't take long before she quickly became a very good surfer.

Because Ricochet had service dog training, she is very comfortable around people with disabilities and she puts them at ease. Today, she helps children and disabled people enjoy the sport of surfing. Ricochet stands on one end of the surfboard and the disabled rider stands on the other end. This balances the board so the rider can stay on the board. She also surfs in competitions as fundraisers for charities. Ricochet didn't make it as a traditional service dog, but today she's a SURFice™ dog.

CULTURE TALK!

In San Francisco, service dogs can go anywhere their owners can go—for example, into restaurants and stores. Is this a good idea?

B Find and underline words that introduce causes and effects in the article. Then answer the questions.
1. Why did Ricochet have to leave the service dog training program?
2. Why did Ricochet's owner think she could learn how to surf?
3. Why is Ricochet good at helping disabled people surf?
4. How does Ricochet help people stay on the surfboard?

C Think about an interesting news event that you recently heard or read about. What happened? What are the causes and effects? Write down notes on a separate piece of paper.

D Write a paragraph about an interesting news event. Use your notes in Part C.

READING
Identifying cause and effect (2)
To answer *Why?* questions, remember to look for the word *because*. Also look for the words *as a result* and *so*.

ONLINE PRACTICE

I can... identify cause and effect in a reading. ☐ Very well ☐ Well ☐ Not very well

UNIT 11   71

5 VIEWING: Junior detective

A You are going to watch a news report about a girl who solved a crime. Look at the two photos. How old do you think the girl is? What kind of crime do you think this was?

B Watch the video. Check ✓ the words below each time you hear them. Then match the words with their definitions.

_d_ 1. suspects   a. something that gives a reason to believe something
___ 2. forced entry   b. marks made by a person's fingers
___ 3. pawn shop   c. a store that buys things from people, and then resells them
___ 4. fingerprints   d. people who other people think committed a crime
___ 5. broke into   e. entered a building illegally, usually to steal something
___ 6. evidence   f. breaking a door or window to go into a building

> **VIEWING**
> **Noticing repeated words**
> Notice nouns that are repeated. They are often key words, and they help you understand what happens in a story.
>
> ONLINE PRACTICE

C Watch again. Number the events in order from *1–6*.

___ Jessica saw a broken window in the garage.
___ Jessica talked to the thief.
___ The boys sold the furniture to a pawn shop.
___ Two boys stole furniture from Jessica's grandmother.
___ Jessica brought evidence to the police.
___ Jessica went to the pawn shop and saw the furniture.

D Do you think Jessica made good decisions? Did she do anything dangerous? Discuss your ideas with a partner.

> **I can...** notice repeated key words.   ☐ Very well   ☐ Well   ☐ Not very well

6 PRESENTING

A Look at the photo. What do you think the news story is about? Share your ideas with a small group.

B Read the presentation. Were your guesses from Part A correct?

> **PRESENTING**
> **Using an anchor image**
> Choose one image to anchor, or focus, your presentation. It should make viewers interested in your story.
>
> ONLINE PRACTICE

66 The government in Wenling, China was building a new highway. There were houses in the way, so officials offered people money to leave their homes. Most residents agreed to move, but for Luo Baogen and his wife, the money wasn't enough. They refused to move out of their five-story apartment building. So officials allowed the Baogens to keep their house, and they built the highway around it. A month later, they offered the Baogens more money. The Baogens finally accepted the offer, and the house was torn down. 99

C Think of an interesting news story or search for one on the Internet. Find a good anchor image. Take notes about the story.

Where did it happen?
When did it happen?
What happened?

D Stand up. Use your anchor image and your notes from Part C to tell your story to a group.

PRESENT

TIP
Show the image to your audience for a few moments before you start speaking.

I can... use an anchor image in a presentation.   ☐ Very well   ☐ Well   ☐ Not very well

73

12 Travel stories

Vocabulary and Listening
Listening for key words (2)
Speaking
Continuing the conversation

Grammar
Present perfect for experiences
Reading and Writing
Self-assessing

Viewing
Using subtitles
Presenting
Using superlatives for emphasis

1 VOCABULARY AND LISTENING

A Listen and repeat.
CD 2-33

1. lose your wallet
2. travel alone 
3. try local food 
4. call room service 
5. visit a local market 
6. exchange currency 
7. miss a flight 
8. ask for directions 

B Complete the story with words from Part A.

I went to Mexico with my friend because I don't like to ¹_____.
On the way to the airport, there was a terrible traffic jam. I thought we were going to
²_____ our ³_____, but we made it. At the hotel, we wanted to
⁴_____, so the hotel concierge recommended a nearby restaurant. We
couldn't find it, so we had to ⁵_____. It was great to practice our Spanish.
Then we decided to ⁶_____. We got some jewelry.

C Listen to people leaving messages while they're traveling.
CD 2-34 Match the person with the situation.

___ 1. Alex   a. can ask for directions
___ 2. David   b. called room service
___ 3. Tracey   c. missed a flight
___ 4. Mike   d. tried local food

> **LISTENING**
> **Listening for key words (2)**
> Notice key words you see in questions before listening. Then listen for the same words to answer the questions.
>
> ONLINE PRACTICE

D Listen Again Answer the questions below about the key words.
CD 2-34
1. When will Alex **call again**?
2. Why is David **tired**?
3. Where did Tracey **eat**?
4. What **lessons** did Mike **take**?

I can... listen for key words in travel stories.   ☐ Very well   ☐ Well   ☐ Not very well

2 SPEAKING

A Put the conversation in order. Number the sentences from *1–6*.

___ Wow, that's even worse!   ___ It was great, but I lost my wallet.

___ Welcome back. How was your trip?   ___ Not my wallet, but I once lost my passport.

___ What do you think happened to it?   ___ I think I left it in a taxi. Has that ever happened to you?

B Listen to the conversation. Then practice with a partner.
CD 2-35

Jill: Have you traveled a lot, Bob?

Bob: Yes, I have. I've been to 30 different countries.

Jill: That's a lot. Have you ever gotten sick on a trip?

Bob: Oh, yes. Accidents, too, but I'll never stop traveling. I've even traveled alone. People are friendly to travelers.

Jill: What's the worst thing that's ever happened to you?

Bob: I lost my passport and I ran out of money one time. **What about you?**

Jill: I lost my wallet once. That's the worst so far. But I've never missed a flight.

SPEAKING
Continuing the conversation

After you answer a question, ask another one. Use phrases like *What about you?* to keep the conversation going.

ONLINE PRACTICE

C Work in pairs. Practice the conversation below with your own information. Continue the conversation.

A: What the worst thing that's ever happened to you while traveling?

B: One time, I _____. What about you?

A: I _____.

CULTURE TALK!

Bangkok, Thailand was the most popular travel destination in 2013. What do you think will be the most popular in ten years? Twenty?

D **Pronunciation** **Stress with content words** Listen and repeat. Content words—nouns and verbs—receive more stress in collocations.
CD 2-36

1. **lose** your **wallet**
2. **ask** for **directions**
3. **miss** a **flight**
4. **visit** a **market**

> **I can...** continue the conversation.   ☐ Very well   ☐ Well   ☐ Not very well

UNIT 12

3 GRAMMAR

A Listen. Then listen again and repeat.

Grammar Reference page 93

Present perfect for experiences	
Have you **tried** the local food?	Yes, I **have**. I've **tried** the local food.
Have you ever **traveled** alone?	Yes, I've **traveled** alone three times.
Have you ever **been** to a local market?	No, I **haven't**. I've never **been** to a local market.
What's the biggest country you've **visited**?	The biggest country I've **visited** is China.
How many times **have** you **missed** a flight?	I've **missed** a flight once.

B Put the words in order to unscramble the sentences.

1. Europe / you / have / visited / ever
   _____?
2. No / taken / never / have / a cruise / I
   _____.
3. ever / Sam / lost / his passport / has
   _____?
4. two times / to Singapore / Remy / been / has
   _____.
5. tried / yet / we / the local food / haven't
   _____.
6. gone / I / on road trips / before / have
   _____.

C Work in pairs. Ask and answer questions. Use the present perfect.

Example:
Josh / many times
A: Has Josh ever visited a local market?
B: Yes, he has. He's visited them many times.

Example:
you / never
A: Have you ever called room service at a hotel?
B: No, I haven't. I've never called room service.

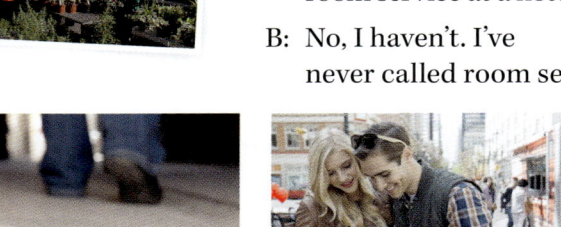

1. you / a few times
2. Mark / never 
3. James and Mariela / couple of times 
4. Roberto / many times 
5. Rick / never 
6. you / many adventures 

D Grammar Talk! Have you ever...? Student A page 102, Student B page 105.

I can... use the present perfect for experiences. ☐ Very well ☐ Well ☐ Not very well

4 READING AND WRITING

A Read and listen. Where did these people travel?

Travel Mishaps

Travel can be frustrating when things go wrong. Here are two travel mishap stories.

Gabriela:

On my second night in Paris, I asked the driver to take me back to my hotel. Unfortunately, he didn't understand me, and I didn't understand him. I gave him the address of the hotel on a piece of paper and he headed off. After we drove around for a couple of hours, I knew he was lost. I called the staff at the hotel myself, who spoke English and French. I put the driver on the phone, and we finally got there at 3:00 in the morning. I was pretty irritated about going to sleep so late.

Rick:

I love New York City, but I once lost my credit card there. I was eating lunch at a café the day before I was going home, and I paid with my credit card because I was running low on cash. When I looked for my card to pay for some shopping later, it wasn't there. The café said they didn't have it, and my card company said it would take 24 hours to get a new card. So, I was stuck in New York with hardly any money for the rest of my stay. Luckily, I had enough money to hop on the subway to go to the airport the next day, but that café lunch was my last meal in Manhattan.

B Answer the questions.
1. Why couldn't Gabriela and the taxi driver communicate?
2. How did the taxi driver finally find Gabriela's hotel?
3. When did Rick lose his credit card?
4. How long did Rick have to wait for a new credit card?
5. Who had a worse travel experience, Gabriela or Rick?

C Think about a trip that went wrong, or use your imagination. What went wrong? Write down notes on a separate piece of paper.

D Write a paragraph about a trip you took, or create a story. Use your notes from Part C. When you finish, self-assess and revise.

WRITING
Self-assessing
After you write, look at how well you've explained your ideas. Then correct spelling and grammar mistakes.

ONLINE PRACTICE

I can... self-assess my writing. ☐ Very well ☐ Well ☐ Not very well

UNIT 12   77

5 VIEWING: Hotel troubles

A Look at the photo and map. What problems do you see with the hotel?

B Watch the video. What is the problem with each hotel? What are the reasons for these problems?

	Jan and Dave	Ann and Jolie
Problems		
Reasons		

CULTURE TALK!

Many people in Turkey go to beach towns, like Bodrum, for vacation. Where do you like to take vacations?

C Watch again. Use the subtitles to complete the sentences.

1. Jan: "It looked _____. Just what we were looking for."
2. Dave: "An adjacent hotel's security guard met us and said that the Club Aqua Hotel had been _____."
3. Jolie: "I was looking forward to the _____."
4. Jolie: "I was really _____. I couldn't believe I was staying in a hotel like that."
5. Ann: "The man at the door asked us to go down to reception to talk to the _____."

**VIEWING
Using subtitles**
If accents are hard to understand, read the subtitles as you listen. This helps you understand the accents.

ONLINE PRACTICE

D Discuss these questions with a partner.

1. What would you do if you were Dave and Jan? Ann and Jolie?
2. What do you think should happen to websites like Travelsoon?

I can... use subtitles to understand a video. ☐ Very well ☐ Well ☐ Not very well

6 PRESENTING

A Read the presentation. Underline the superlative forms.

> PRESENTING
> **Using superlatives for emphasis**
> Use superlative forms (*most* or *-est*) in your presentation to say something in a more engaging or powerful way.
>
> ONLINE PRACTICE

> 66 When I was in college, I went on a trip to Disney World with my friends. It was the best trip I've ever taken, but also the most expensive. We stayed at a really nice condo with the biggest water slides I've ever seen. We went to a different park every day. They were all great, but the Harry Potter park was the most fun. Because we traveled in the off season, the parks weren't too crowded. The weather was perfect. And we had no travel problems — the flights were on time, and the airline didn't lose our luggage. It was the greatest vacation ever. 99

B Read the presentation in Part A to a partner. Stress the superlative forms.

C Think about the best or worst trip you've ever taken. Answer these questions.

Where did you go?

When did you go?

Who did you go with?

What did you do?

Why was it your best or worst travel experience?

D Stand up. Use your notes from Part C to tell a group about your trip. Remember to use superlative forms.

PRESENT

TIP

Pronounce *the* as *thee* before the superlative forms for more emphasis.

> **I can...** use superlatives for emphasis. ☐ Very well   ☐ Well   ☐ Not very well

79

Self-Assessment

1 VOCABULARY

Circle the correct word or words to complete each sentence.

1. This book is about two people who get married. It's a mystery / *romance* / western.
2. I'm reading a *historical fiction* / fantasy / mystery novel about a family that lived in New York in the 1800s.
3. This western / biography / *science fiction book* talks about visitors from other planets.
4. I want to read a *biography* / fantasy / romance about Albert Einstein. I'm interested in learning about his life.

I can... understand vocabulary about stories. (Unit 10)

5. The police are solving three *crimes* / floods / demonstrations in the neighborhood this week.
6. Did you vote in the exhibition / demonstration / *election* yesterday?
7. It's going to rain all week. I think there's going to be a crime / exhibition / *flood*.

I can... understand vocabulary about the news. (Unit 11)

8. Not all stores take credit or debit cards. Tourists should *exchange currency* / call room service / visit a local market before traveling.
9. The weather was terrible. So we just stayed in our hotel and *called room service* / tried local food / visited a local market.
10. There was a lot of traffic on the way to the airport. We were so late, we almost asked for directions / called room service / *missed our flight*.

I can... understand vocabulary about travel stories. (Unit 12)

2 GRAMMAR

1. She told / *told me* / said me she was tired.
2. He *asked me if* / asks me / asked me I had been to London.
3. He told me they seen / have seen / *had seen* a science fiction movie last night.

I can... use reported speech. (Unit 10)

4. Jack stopped by while I *was cooking* / cooked / am cooking dinner.
5. I wasn't here when Trish was arriving / arrives / *arrived*.
6. The storm began while we waiting / *were waiting* / waited for the bus.

I can... use *while* and *when* clauses. (Unit 11)

7. Are / *Have* / Has you ever missed a flight?
8. *I've never called* / 's never called / 've never call room service.
9. Sara traveled / have traveled / *has traveled* alone several times.
10. You losing / 's lost / *'ve lost* your wallet twice.

I can... use the present perfect for experiences. (Unit 12)

80

Units 10-12

3 READING

A Read and listen to the article. In what year was the ring lost?

Lost Ring Appears 72 Years Later

Imagine losing a ring one day and getting it back 72 years later. It sounds like science fiction, but this really happened to a man named Jesse Taylor Mattos. In 1938, Mattos was at work one day in Dunsmuir, California, when he accidentally dropped his high school class ring in a toilet and flushed it away. Thinking that it was lost forever, Mattos forgot all about it.

In 2010, a city worker named Tony Congi was cleaning the city's sewer lines when he saw something shiny on top of a pile of dirt. He picked it up and saw the words "Class of 1938" and the initials "J.T.M." on the inside of the ring.

Congi went to the same high school as Mattos. Congi looked through a yearbook from 1938 and found a photo of Jesse Mattos, and noticed that he was the only graduate with the initials J.T.M. Congi found one of Mattos's classmates who was friends with Mattos and had his phone number.

Congi traveled to where Mattos lived and reunited Mattos with his high school ring. While they were chatting, the two men shared information about their lives in Dunsmuir and learned that Congi grew up next door to Mattos's sister. Mattos's sister even babysat Congi a few times when he was a baby.

Congi has found hundreds of coins, old spoons, and pieces of jewelry in the sewers, but this is the first time he felt that he found a real treasure.

B Answer each question with information from the article.
1. What was Congi doing when he found the ring?
2. What do the initials J.T.M. stand for?
3. How many lost items has Congi found in the sewer?
4. Why do you think the writer compares this story with science fiction?
5. What would you do if you lost an important ring? How would you feel?

C Imagine you are Congi and are about to meet Mattos to return his ring. What would you say? Describe the conversation between the two men.

SELF-ASSESSMENT | UNITS 10-12   81

GRAMMAR REFERENCE

Unit 7

Present perfect continuous and present perfect

We can use the present perfect to talk about something that began in the past and has just finished, or something that happened at an indefinite time or many indefinite times in the past.

We use the present perfect continuous to talk about an action that began in the past and continues to the present.

Present perfect continuous			Present perfect		
I You We They	have	been	reading all day. running all day. writing all day. drawing all day.	I You We They	have	read five books already. run two miles already. written ten pages already. drawn eight pictures already.
He She (It)	has			He She (It)	has	

Grammar Practice!

1 Complete the conversations with the present perfect or present perfect continuous forms of the verbs in parentheses.

1. A: _____ lately? (what / you / do)
   B: I've been working a lot.
2. A: Do you want some pizza?
   B: No thanks. _____ five slices already. (I / eat)
3. A: You look tired.
   B: _____ since 6:00 this morning. (I / study)
4. A: _____ to Japan? (how many times / you / be)
   B: About five times.
5. A: I didn't know you practice martial arts.
   B: Yup. _____ martial arts since I was five years old. (I / practice)

2 Complete the conversation with the present perfect or present perfect continuous forms of the verbs in parentheses.

A: What _____ lately? (you / do)
B: I have a test next week, so I _____ all day. (study)
A: _____ the teacher how many questions there will be? (you / ask)
B: Yes, but he _____ creating the test yet. (not / finish)
A: Well, you look tired. _____ any sleep? (you / get)
B: Not really. I _____ a lot of coffee. (drink)
A: How many cups _____ so far? (you / have)
B: I just finished my tenth cup. I need to get some more!

Unit 8

Used to

We use the base form of a verb with *used to* for something that was true in the past but is no longer true anymore. We use *used to* in affirmative statements and *use to* in questions and negative statements. We use the same form for all subjects.

Affirmative statements		Negative statements	
I He She It You We They	**used to have** long hair.	I He She It You We They	**didn't use to have** short hair.

Yes/No Questions			Questions with *How*			
Did	I he she it you we they	**use to work** here?	**How**	**did**	I he she it you we they	**use to get** to work?

Grammar Practice!

1 Complete the sentences with the correct form of *used to* and the verbs in parentheses.
1. Frank and I _____ together. (work)
2. Wendy _____ in this class. (not / be)
3. How did you _____ in touch with friends? (keep)
4. I didn't _____ confident. (look)
5. Sam _____ guitar lessons. (take)

2 Rewrite these sentences and questions with the correct form of *used to*.
1. Sheila lived near me. _____.
2. Luke didn't have a mustache. _____.
3. Karen rode the bus to school. _____.
4. Did Anna look scruffy? _____?
5. How did you go to school? _____?

GRAMMAR REFERENCE 89

Unit 9

Questions with *How long*

We can use *how long* to ask questions with the simple past, the present perfect and the present perfect continuous.

In questions with *how long*, the present perfect and the present perfect continuous have the same basic meaning. However, we often use the present perfect continuous when we want to talk about the duration, or how long the activity lasted.

Some verbs, such as *be, like, love, want, need,* and *know,* cannot be used with continuous tenses.

Simple past	How long **did** you **work** here?	From 2002 to 2007. I work somewhere else now.	How long **did** you **know** her?	For two years. Then she moved to Japan.
Present perfect	How long **have** you **worked** here?	For ten years. I love working here.	How long **have** you **known** her?	For five years. We live together now.
Present perfect continuous	How long **have** you **been working** here?		~~How long have you **been knowing** her?~~	

Grammar Practice!

1 Change the sentences below into questions with *How long* and the correct tense.

1. We've been walking all day.
   _____?

2. I slept a lot last night.
   _____?

3. Kyle's been cleaning his house for a while.
   _____?

4. She's been taking pictures of endangered species since 2005.
   _____?

5. Tyler sang to the audience for an hour.
   _____?

2 Complete each question with *How long* and the correct form of the verb in parentheses.

1. A: _____ in nursing school? (you / be)
   B: For two years. I graduated last year.
2. A: _____? (Thomas / study)
   B: He's been studying all day.
3. A: _____ Kendra? (you / know)
   B: Since we were ten. We're really good friends.
4. A: _____ that bike? (you / want)
   B: I've wanted it since last summer.
5. A: _____ a teacher? (Sam / be)
   B: For about three years. He loves being a teacher.

Unit 10

Reported speech

We use reported speech to report something that someone else has said. In reported speech, we usually change the speaker's verb tense.

simple present	→	simple past
present progressive	→	past progressive
simple past	→	past perfect
present perfect	→	past perfect

We use *said* or *told* + noun/pronoun to introduce reported speech in statements.

We use *asked if* + noun/pronoun to introduce reported speech in questions.

Note how the order of verbs changes to subject + verb in questions.

- My mother asked me if **I was** doing my homework.
  NOT
- My mother asked me if ~~was I~~ doing my homework.

Direct statements	Reported statements
He said, "My book **is** really good."	He **said / told me** his book **was** really good.
She said, "I**'m walking** to work."	She **said / told me** she **was walking** to work.
They said, "We **went** out of town."	They **said / told me** they**'d gone** out of town.
She said, "I**'ve been** there twice."	She **said / told us** she**'d been** there twice.

Direct questions	Reported questions
She asked, "**Do** you **like** mysteries?"	She **asked me if** I **liked** mysteries.
He asked, "**Are** you **studying**?"	He **asked us if** we **were studying**.
She asked, "**Did** you **pass** the test?"	She **asked me if** I **had passed** the test.
He asked, "**Has** Ken **seen** the movie?"	He **asked me if** Ken **had seen** the movie.

Grammar Practice!

1 Circle the correct words to complete the reported statements and questions.

1. "We're really busy." → He said they *were / have been* really busy.
2. "Do you have the book with you?" → She asked me if I *have / had* the book with me.
3. "I haven't gone to Tokyo." → He told me he *didn't go / hadn't gone* to Tokyo.
4. "I called Marilyn." → She told me she *has called / had called* Marilyn.
5. "Are they driving to L.A.?" → He asked if they *had been driving / were driving* to L.A.

2 Complete each reported statement or question with the correct form of the bold verb.

1. "I**'m** tired." → He said _____ tired.
2. "We **arrived** on time." → She said _____ on time.
3. "I **haven't seen** Karen today." → She told me _____ Karen today.
4. "**Is** Jack **staying** with you?" → He asked me if _____ with me.
5. "Do you **have** the time?" → She asked me if _____ the time.

GRAMMAR REFERENCE   91

Unit 11

While and *when* clauses

We use *when* before the simple past.

- *He was studying **when** the phone **rang**.*

We use *while* before the past progressive.

- *The phone rang **while** he was **studying**.*

In a sentence with two past progressive clauses and *while*, the two events were happening at the same time.

In a sentence with two simple past clauses and *when*, the event after *when* happened first.

In a sentence with a past progressive and a simple past clause, the simple past event interrupted the past progressive event. The past progressive event started first and was already in progress when the simple past event happened

Sentence	First Event	Second Event
I was listening to music **while** I was jogging.	same time	same time
I was jogging **when** it started to rain.	I was jogging.	It started to rain.
I fell **while** it was raining.	It was raining.	I fell.
When I fell, I called for help.	I fell.	I called for help.

Grammar Practice!

1 Circle the correct answer that best describes the underlined event.

1. I was driving home from work when <u>I had a car accident</u>.
    a. first event   b. second event   c. same time
2. I called Margo while <u>I was watching TV</u>.
    a. first event   b. second event   c. same time
3. <u>Nina burned herself</u> while she was cooking.
    a. first event   b. second event   c. same time
4. Ken cheered when <u>his team won the game</u>.
    a. first event   b. second event   c. same time
5. <u>We weren't texting</u> while we were driving.
    a. first event   b. second event   c. same time

2 Combine the two sentences with *when* or *while*.

1. She was taking management classes. She was working in an office.
    _____

2. I was traveling. I got sick.
    _____

3. We weren't paying attention. We were watching the show.
    _____

4. I found a great jacket. I asked for the price.
    _____

5. The manager walked into the meeting room. Everyone stopped talking.
    _____

Unit 12

Present perfect for experiences

We can use the present perfect to talk about events that began in the past and continue to the present.

- *How long* **have** you **been** *here?*   *I've* **been** *here for five years.*

We can also use it to talk about events that happened at an unspecified time or at multiple unspecified times in the past.

- **Have** *you* **ever visited** *Rome?*   *We've* **visited** *Rome many times.*

The present perfect is also used with *ever* and *never* to talk about events that did not happen yet, but could possibly happen in the future.

- **Has** *she* **ever had** *Japanese food?*   *She's* **never had** *Japanese food.*

We often use the present perfect to introduce background information for things that are happening at the moment. For example, we use the present perfect to talk about past experiences that are connected and related to present situations.

Present perfect	Present situation
I've given many presentations before.	Believe me. There's nothing to worry about.
She's worked with children for 20 years.	She has the skills to be a great teacher.
It has never done that before.	I don't know why it's doing it now.
They haven't eaten yet.	They're really hungry.

Grammar Practice!

1 Correct the mistakes in each sentence below.
1. I never have met him before.
2. Has your mother cooking Moroccan tagine before?
3. You have worked in marketing before?
4. I has never been to this restaurant before.
5. She haven't seen a doctor yet.

2 Complete the conversations below with the correct present perfect sentences from Part A.
1. A: _____
   B: Me neither. I wonder what he looks like.
2. A: My mom is a great cook. She just got a job as a chef in a restaurant.
   B: _____
3. A: Is Margo feeling better? Does she know what's wrong with her leg?
   B: No, she doesn't. _____
4. A: _____
   B: No, this is my first marketing job.
5. A: What's delicious here?
   B: I don't know. _____

GRAMMAR REFERENCE   93

Grammar Talk!

7 How many times has Rosa gone horseback riding?
STUDENT A

Ask questions about Rosa with Student B to complete the calendar.

A: What's Rosa been doing?
B: She's been going horseback riding.
A: How many times has she gone horseback riding this week?
B: She's gone horseback riding two times this week.
A: On which days?

Rosa's MyCal — Week of March 1						
Sunday	Monday	Tuesday	Wednesday	Thursday	Friday	Saturday
gardening	websites	websites	websites	websites	websites	___
___	___	___	___	___	___	sports on TV
sports on TV	___	sports on TV	gardening	___	___	___

8 Did she use to have long hair?
STUDENT A

Look at the family portraits. Choose a person. Ask and answer questions with Student B to guess the people you chose. Use *used to*.

A: Did she use to have long hair?
B: No, she didn't. She used to have short hair.
A: Is it Jenny?
B: Yes, it's Jenny.

2005   Now

100

9 How long has she been getting up early?
STUDENT A

Ask and answer questions with Student B about their family members and friends. Use *How long...?*

A: Who gets up early?
B: My sister.
A: How long has she been getting up early?
B: For 2 years.

Habit / Activity	Name	How long...?
get up early		
do chores normally		
go to bed late		
study English		
take out the trash		

10 Do you like historical fiction?
STUDENT A

Ask and answer questions with different classmates about their preferences to complete the chart. Then tell Student B about your conversations.

    A: Do you like historical fiction?
Maria: Yes, I do.
    A: Why?
Maria: I learn a lot.
    A: I asked Maria if she liked historical fiction. She said/told me she liked it because she learns a lot.

Types of Books	Name	Why?
historical fiction		
mysteries		
romance novels		
science fiction		
biographies		

GRAMMAR TALK!

11 What was Manolo doing when the lights went out?
STUDENT A

Ask and answer questions with Student B to complete the chart. Use *while* and *when*.

A: What was Manolo doing when the lights went out?
B: He was studying for an exam.

Person	Activity	News Event
Manolo		the lights go out
Stephanie	eat at a restaurant	the earthquake hit
James		a robber hold up bank
Tim and Mark	watch TV	the Olympic Games start
Claudia		the flood waters approach
Rob and Maria	sleep	fire alarm go off

12 Have you ever missed a flight?
STUDENT A

Ask and answer questions with Student B to complete the chart. Use the present perfect with *ever*, *never*, and *yet*.

A: Have you ever missed a flight?
B: Yes, I have. I missed one while I was coming back from London in 2008.

Experiences	Yes / No	More details
miss a flight		
lose your wallet		
lose your passport		
travel alone		
take a cruise		
run out of money		
try local food		
visit a local market		

7 How many times has Rosa gone horseback riding?
STUDENT B

Ask questions about Rosa with Student A to complete the calendar.

A: What's Rosa been doing?
B: She's been going horseback riding.
A: How many times has she gone horseback riding this week?
B: She's gone horseback riding two times this week.
A: On which days?

Rosa's MyCal — Week of March 1						
Sunday	Monday	Tuesday	Wednesday	Thursday	Friday	Saturday
___	___	___	___	___	___	horseback riding
horseback riding	a concert	martial arts	martial arts	martial arts	martial arts	___
___	___	___	___	a concert	___	a concert

8 Did she use to have long hair?
STUDENT B

Look at the family portraits. Choose a person. Ask and answer questions with Student A to guess the people you chose. Use *used to*.

A: Did she use to have long hair?
B: No, she didn't. She used to have short hair.
A: Is it Jenny?
B: Yes, it's Jenny.

2005

Now

GRAMMAR TALK! 103

9 How long has she been getting up early?
STUDENT B

Ask and answer questions with Student A about their family members and friends. Use *How long...?*

A: Who gets up early?
B: My sister.
A: How long has she been getting up early?
B: For 2 years.

Habit / Activity	Name	How long...?
get up early		
do chores normally		
go to bed late		
study English		
take out the trash		

10 Do you like historical fiction?
STUDENT B

Ask and answer questions with different classmates about their preferences to complete the chart. Then tell Student A about your conversations.

A: Do you like historical fiction?
Maria: Yes, I do.
A: Why?
Maria: I learn a lot.
A: I asked Maria if she liked historical fiction. She said/told me she liked it because she learns a lot.

Types of Books	Name	Why?
historical fiction		
mysteries		
romance novels		
science fiction		
biographies		

11 What was Manolo doing when the lights went out?
STUDENT B

Ask and answer questions with Student A to complete the chart. Use *while* and *when*.

A: What was Manolo doing when the lights went out?
B: He was studying for an exam.

Person	Activity	News Event
Manolo	study for an exam	the lights go out
Stephanie		the earthquake hit
James	use the ATM	a robber hold up bank
Tim and Mark		the Olympic Games start
Claudia	work in the yard	the flood waters approach
Rob and Maria		fire alarm go off

12 Have you ever missed a flight?
STUDENT B

Ask and answer questions with Student A to complete the chart. Use the present perfect with *ever*, *never*, and *yet*.

A: Have you ever missed a flight?
B: Yes, I have. I missed one while I was coming back from London in 2008.

Experiences	Yes / No	More details
miss a flight		
lose your wallet		
lose your passport		
travel alone		
take a cruise		
run out of money		
try local food		
visit a local market		

GRAMMAR TALK!

WORD LIST

Unit 7
VOCABULARY
go horseback riding
catch up with friends
practice martial arts
build a website
go to concerts
go to flea markets
do gardening
have brunch

READING VOCABULARY
day-long
full bloom
stage presence
old pals
shut-eye

Unit 8
VOCABULARY
mustache
wavy hair
bald
beard
scruffy
neat
confident
studious

USEFUL PHRASES
I know.
That's true.
You're right.

READING VOCABULARY
weigh in
remarkable
goof off
dapper
indifferent

Unit 9
VOCABULARY
get up early
use an alarm
do chores
ride a bike to school
go to bed late
check my messages
catch up on the news
take out the trash

USEFUL PHRASES
Tell me about…

READING VOCABULARY
animator
fixer-upper
materials
bohemian
junk

Unit 10
VOCABULARY
mystery
science fiction
western
biography
romance
fantasy
historical fiction
children's literature

USEFUL PHRASES
Sorry, but…
Maybe we can…

READING VOCABULARY
explorer
expeditions
commanded
fleet
trade

Unit 11
VOCABULARY
flood
fire
crime
demonstration
election
sports event
fashion show
exhibition

READING VOCABULARY
disabled
tasks
put at ease
balance
fundraisers

Unit 12
VOCABULARY
lose your wallet
travel alone
try local food
call room service
visit a local market
exchange currency
miss a flight
ask for directions

USEFUL PHRASES
What about you?

READING VOCABULARY
mishaps
head off
irritated
run low
hop on

AUDIO AND VIDEO SCRIPTS

Unit 7 LISTENING page 42

1.
A: So, what have you been doing since you moved to the city?
B: Well, I've been listening to a lot of live music in the park.
A: Me, too. Maybe we can go together sometime.

2.
A: When did you ride for the first time?
B: About ten years ago, when I got my first horse.
A: How many horses have you had?

3.
A: It's wonderful training for the mind and the body. I earned my black belt when I was 15.
B: How long have you been practicing?

4.
A: How long have you been building your site?
B: For over a month now, and I still haven't finished it. But it's really fun and creative. Have you finished yours yet?

Unit 7 VIDEO page 46

Narrator: In the world of Chinese opera, everything from the makeup to the style of singing can seem mysterious to people from different cultures.
Woman: OK, say cheese.
Tyler: Cheese.
N: So how did ten-year-old Tyler Thompson of Oakland, California become a Chinese opera star? He sings beautifully in a language he doesn't even speak.
Girl 1: I was like, "Wow, he's pretty good."
Girl 2: Oh, he's so cute.
Woman 2: The pronunciation is quite correct. Yeah. M-hm. Very good, yeah.
Tyler: Singing pretty much runs in the family. My dad sings, my mom sings, my grandmother sings.
I: But I bet you're the only one on your block who sings in Chinese.
Tyler: Yup.
N: The Purple Bamboo Orchestra was started by Sherlyn Chew.
Sherlyn: Leave it up there until they're done.
N: She's part music director. Part singing coach. Part second mom.
Sherlyn: You know, spit out the gum, spit out the candy.
N: She started the orchestra to teach children about their Chinese culture, to keep an old culture alive in a new country. Now, it's part of Tyler's culture, too. Tyler and his classmate, Carol Liu, have been working on a duet.
Tyler: It's like, when we sing together, it's like one voice on one side, one voice on the other. Soon, it could become one. One whole voice.
Woman 3: Wonderful, so nice. You must be very proud.
Tyler's mom: Thank you.
N: Now, Tyler has become a star at Chinese opera performances all over California. The audience members are not all Chinese. Part of Sherlyn Chew's mission with the Purple Bamboo Orchestra is to share her culture.
Sherlyn: When we leave Chinatown, you know, we are promoting our culture. If we stay in Chinatown, we're only preserving it.
I: What do you think the people in China thought, seeing you singing Chinese opera?
Carol: I think I know.
I: What do you think?
Carol: Well, amazed.
N: And people are amazed that an energetic ten-year-old has become a bridge between two cultures.

Unit 7 PRESENTING page 47

My brother is an autograph hound, or "grapher." In his free time, he likes to get the autographs of famous people. He goes online to buy baseball cards and photos of baseball players and other athletes. Then he goes to sports games and asks players to sign his cards, photos, or baseballs. Once in a while, he also gets autographs from other famous people such as singers, actors, and politicians. He sells or trades some of the autographed items online. He's been graphing since he was about twelve years old. I think it's a silly hobby, but it makes him happy.

Unit 8 LISTENING page 48

1.
A: So tell me about the new manager. Is he that wavy-haired, confident-looking guy I've seen in the cafeteria?
B: I'm afraid not. He doesn't look very confident, and he doesn't have wavy hair. He's bald, and he has a big mustache.

2.
A: Is that Jay's brother, the scruffy guy with the mustache?
B: You're looking at the wrong person. His brother is standing next to Jay, the neat one with the beard.

3.
A: Alison's very neat and studious, or so I've heard.
B: Well, she's very studious. That's true. But who said she's neat? She's one of the messiest people I know.

4.
A: The tour guide's kind of scruffy-looking, isn't he?
B: Yeah, he is, but he's very confident. Even though he isn't very organized, he's doing a great job.

Unit 8 VIDEO page 52

Lisa: I can hardly bear to look at you. Right. What do you see when you look in the mirror now, with that?
Stuart: Huge!
Lisa: The arms don't fit you.
Stuart: No.
Lisa: The jacket's way too long.
Mica: The cut of the leg is just completely wrong.
Lisa: Follow me.
N: These men will need a firm hand when it comes to their style rules.
Mica: Take a look at this. Don't laugh. Who are these two? You see that these two guys have the same thing in common. They're both short, but they are loved by millions and millions and millions of women. They haven't allowed their height to restrict them. This is where you're going to get to. This is what you're going to be.
Lisa: Cool. Now, Stuart, make sure when you go shopping, the sweater you buy has a V-neck 'cause I know you like to have your necklines up here.
Stuart: Right.
Lisa: But it's not flattering, OK? Nice bright sweater, but a fine knit. Nothing too heavy, 'cause it's only going to bulk you out. As you see, the color comes underneath the sweater as well, from the T-shirt, and that's going to be the smallest part of you, across here. This is your other look. When you go shopping, maybe not everything's going to fit you correctly. So, you need to think about maybe having a few things altered. We're going to stay away from black. That's why I've gone for this brown color.
N: This is the first time Stuart will have seen his whole new look put together.
Mica: So, handsome. Mm, my goodness, you look good.
Lisa: One, two, three.
Stuart: Oh, wow.
Mica: You just look amazing.
Mica: Have you ever seen yourself look this good?
Stuart: No.
Mica: So, what has this done for your whole confidence level?
Stuart: It's just absolutely gone through the roof. Now I'm looking in the mirror going yeah, I'm, I'm a handsome devil.
Mica: Oooh!
Lisa: Such a cool dude!
Mica: Look at that! My goodness.
Lisa: I'm looking at you and your whole face is lit up. You have

AUDIO AND VIDEO SCRIPTS   111

that twinkle in your eye, and you look genuinely, really happy.
Stuart: I can't believe it's me, looking back at me. You know, I look ten years, twenty years younger. And I feel young again.

Unit 9 LISTENING page 54

1. I almost always go to bed after midnight. I've tried to go to bed earlier, but I just lie there with my eyes open. It's no use!
2. I never used to like cycling, but now I'm really into it. I think it's great. I ride my bike to school every day.
3. I like to get my work done early. I get up at 6:00 a.m. almost every day and do all my homework. Then it's all out of the way for the rest of the day!
4. Everyone in my family does household chores every Sunday afternoon. Everyone except my little sister, who's only two months old.

Unit 9 VIDEO page 58

Narrator: At the StrawberryFrog agency in New York City, why is this employee sleeping? And what's that she's sleeping in? This salesman wants these people to… nap? That's right. He's trying to persuade managers at StrawberryFrog to let their employees nap at work.
Salesman: So, if he's snoring, hopefully the person sitting over there won't really hear it.
Jo: Just because you're working all day does not mean that you're going to get good productivity out of your staff.
N: Jo Pugh, who is one of the managers, put this napping pod in a corner of this busy office.
Interviewer: Someone might come in with pajamas.
Jo: Maybe they will.
I: Would that be OK?
Jo: That would, I think, be fine.
Salesman: Set the timer.
N: The company that sold the pod to StrawberryFrog also has its own napping rooms: $14 for 20 minutes. They tell bosses: employers let workers take coffee breaks, so why not sleeping breaks?
I: In other countries, this such as
Jo: No. You got a *siesta*. You know? The *siesta* in southern Europe. You know, places don't grind to a halt just because people are having an afternoon lie-down.
N: Napping pods are becoming popular. One study of twenty-four hour companies shows more than fifteen percent encourage napping during work hours. At StrawberryFrog, employees love the pods and managers report that their workers' productivity has gone up.
Man: We all slow down at various points in the day. It's the time that we look at the nearest couch and think, "If only…" Science shows that having a nap can revive a tired mind, and so does history.
N: John F. Kennedy, Lyndon B. Johnson, Eleanor Roosevelt, and Leonardo da Vinci all napped. Maybe the most famous napper was Winston Churchill, who used this bed at work for his daily nap. Jo Pugh quickly became a pod person herself. She says that her daily twenty-minute has given her a lot more energy.

Unit 10 LISTENING page 62

1. Paul Cézanne was born on January 19, 1839 in Aix-en-Provence, where he went to school. He studied law there from 1859 to 1861. At the same time, he attended drawing classes. In 1861, he decided he wanted to be a painter and moved to Paris.
2. It was high noon when the stranger rode into the dusty little town of Silver Rush. He rode in confidently on a big white horse. He was wearing tall leather boots and a white hat, with ropes and a gun in each hand. What was he doing here? Did he come here to work—or to cause trouble?
3. The moon was full and the night sky was full of stars. The ocean waves were lapping on the beach as a band was playing soft music in the café behind them. He took her hand in his. "Darling," he said. "I can't live without you. Will you marry me?"
4. Humans have been exploring the galaxy for about 70 years, since 2053. Our ships have found many habitable planets. My ship, the Venture II, has surveyed more than 100 planets. We have found many forms of life—animals, insects, and plants. But we haven't found any intelligent living beings that we can communicate with.

Unit 10 VIDEO page 66

Narrator: Stephen King is the king of horror books. Since 1974, he has written fifty novels, almost two hundred scary short stories, and five nonfiction books. King writes for at least four hours every day, except on his birthday and important holidays.
Stephen King: The ideas come, and they have to be let out, that's all. They just have to be let out.
N: King wants to scare us. But what scares *him*?
King: Everything that scares you. Everything that scares anybody. That's part of the reason for my success.
N: Stephen King and his wife Tabitha met in college. They've been married for twenty-six years, and they have raised three children. And because Tabitha is also a writer, they understand each other.
Tabitha: I don't find what he writes weird and I don't find his characters weird, OK? I really, I think one of his tremendous appeals to people is that he puts you in a world that you recognize, among people that you know, and then if bizarre things happen to them, well, the world is a very strange place.
N: Stephen doesn't spend all of his time writing, though. He's in a band with a group of other famous writers who sing. He is also a big baseball fan. He even built a million-dollar baseball park for kids behind his house.
Man: Good job!
Interviewer: You're kind of a kid.
King: Yeah.
N: King was born in Portland, Maine, in 1947. He says his childhood was normal. He started writing when he was a kid and sold his first story to a magazine when he was eighteen. After Stephen and Tabitha got married, they lived in a cheap apartment. She worked at a donut shop. He worked at a laundry. But he kept writing, and one day in 1973, his editor called. Paperback rights for *Carrie* sold for four hundred thousand dollars. Today, the Kings have enough money to rebuild the local library. Stephen says he has always loved to read.
I: Do you like Jane Austen?
King: I've never read a Jane Austen novel in my life. Seen a couple of the movies. Aah, you don't put that on the air.
I: Tolstoy — did you, have…
King: I've never read Tolstoy.
I: You've never read Jane Austen or Tolstoy?
King: Never read Jane Austen or Tolstoy.
I: The greatest novelists.
King: I've read most of what Dean Koontz has written, though.
I: Here you are, one of the best-selling authors in all of history, and the critics can't find much that they like in your work. Does this hurt?
King: Well, it does hurt.
N: But his fans don't seem to care what his critics say. They love his books.

Unit 11 LISTENING page 68

1. A show of photographs by Edwin Brook opened at the Metropolitan Museum yesterday. Many of the photographer's most famous images are among the 60 photos on display. Over 800 people showed up for the opening, which will continue until the 31st of this month.
2. Bibi Martin showed her new collection at the Mode XM show in London this week, held at Dorchester House on Friday evening. Top London models showed off Ms. Martin's new designs. The event featured live

112

music, and a host of local celebrities showed up to enjoy the show.
3. Amy Madden, Boston University tennis player, won the CTA Championship at the East Side Tennis Club in New York on Sunday. She defeated Serena Smith from Emory University in the finals. Madden is the first Boston University player to win the CTA Championship.
4. Police are investigating a break-in at the CenterCorp headquarters that occurred last night. Laptops and several flat-screen monitors were stolen, along with documents that were in locked file drawers. Police suspect that a recently fired employee might be responsible for the burglary.

Unit 11 VIDEO page 72

Male newscaster: She had no plans to be a crime fighter herself, at least not at this age.
Female newscaster: No, but you know, things happen. Someone broke into her great-grandmother's home, and not only did Jessica get her stuff back, but she actually tracked down one of the suspects. Jessica Maple joins us this morning with her story. Jessica, great to have you with us. So the police initially said, you know, no sign of forced entry, and you said, "Wait a minute. This doesn't make sense. I know there's more to the story." You go down to your great-grandmother's house. Walk us through what happened next.
Jessica: Well, when I went to my grandmother's house, I went to the garage and I saw there was broken glass on the garage window and there were fingerprints everywhere. So then I thought, hmm, there's no forced point of entry. I'm looking at it right now. So, there is an obvious sign of forced entry, and so then my mother and I, we opened the garage, and we go inside the house, and there's clothing all over the place. And did I mention that the furniture was gone?
Female newscaster: Everything was gone, right?
Jessica: Yeah!
Male newscaster: Jessica, how old are you again?
Jessica: I'm twelve.
Male newscaster: Are you sure?
Jessica: Yes.
Male newscaster: I want to investigate that! OK, so you find out all the furniture is gone, and your first thought is, "Hey, let's go downtown and let's check out some of the pawn shops to see if anybody's trying to sell this stuff." How did you come up with that idea?
Jessica: Well, I thought to myself, since this is a bad economy, people are going to want money instead of keeping the furniture. And I know that pawn shops, they give you money for giving stuff to, well, selling stuff to them and all. So then, there was a pawn shop that was down the street from my grandmother's house. And my mother and I, we went down there, and we saw like, almost all of my grandmother's furniture in there.
Female newscaster: So, you find all the furniture, they of course have a record of the people who brought it in to pawn it. And so at what point did you call the police and say, um, "I think I may have solved the, uh, issue of the robbery at my grandmother's,"?
Jessica: I called them immediately after I got, I talked to the manager of the pawn shop, and he gave me two pieces of paper that had I.D.s, and it was two guys who broke into my grandmother's house. They were both seventeen, and I talked to the police. I said, "Here's some evidence with the guys' addresses and all that stuff on there. You can go and arrest them now."
Male newscaster: What did the cop say when you brought this evidence to him?
Jessica: He thought to himself, "Wow, you beat me here," and I was like, "I did your job again."
Male newscaster: Hey, we only have a couple of seconds left. I know you confronted the suspects, and they hadn't been arrested yet. What did the kids say when you came up to them and said "Look, I gotcha,"?
Jessica: Well, the guy was standing next to his mom, and so he looked pretty harmless. So then, like, I started asking him questions, like, "How old are you?" uh, like, "What school do you go to?" and all, and then he finally —
Male newscaster: We got to cut you off, Jessica. I'm sorry. Great job, continued success. Nice job, hon.

Unit 12 LISTENING page 74

1. Mom, it's Alex. I'm calling from the airport. Listen, I'm sorry, but I won't be home tonight. I was a little late, and the plane took off without me. There won't be another one until tomorrow afternoon at 4:40. I'll call you again tomorrow morning. Bye!
2. Hi, Dad. It's David. We're having a fantastic time. The weather's great, and we're just relaxing at the hotel room. We just ordered some food from the hotel's restaurant because we're tired from all the walking and sightseeing.
3. Hi, Mom. Hi, Dad. It's Tracey. I wanted to tell you about dinner last night. I was getting tired of fast food, so I decided to eat at a local restaurant. It was delicious and so different from the food back home. Well, just wanted to let you know. I'll call again soon.
4. Hi, Dad. It's Mike. I'm getting along great here. I can ask all sorts of questions, and sometimes even understand the answers. And you know what a bad sense of direction I have. Well, I haven't gotten lost even once on this trip, thanks to those Japanese lessons I took.

Unit 12 VIDEO page 78

Narrator: These people all planned their vacations through an online company called Travelsoon. Dave and Jan Brooks made their reservations after seeing a hotel on the website that looked perfect.
Jan: It looked amazing. Just what we were looking for. I saw quite an idyllic place with a nice pool, and the rooms looked good and comfortable and clean.
N: So in May, they flew to Turkey. After a five-hour delay at the airport, they landed in the middle of the night, and immediately got on a bus to their hotel.
Dave: We found the Club Aqua Hotel, and an adjacent hotel security guard met us and said that the Club Aqua Hotel had been closed.
N: The hotel was closed for renovations. But no one had told Jan and Dave that, and now they had nowhere to stay. The Brooks asked a taxi driver to help them find a hotel and when they found a new one, they had to pay for it themselves. The next morning, Dave called Travelsoon to tell them what had happened. They were moved to a different hotel. But it wasn't what they'd chosen, and it was in a different part of town. But things were even worse for Ann MacKay and her daughter Jolie when they booked a vacation on the same Travelsoon site.
Jolie: Nice sauna. I was looking forward to the holiday.
N: It seemed like they'd found the perfect place, The Royal Panacea Hotel in Turkey. When they got to the hotel, it seemed wonderful.
Jolie: I was really impressed. I couldn't believe I was staying in a hotel like that.
N: The hotel was big, comfortable, and luxurious. But just a few hours later, a man came to their hotel room.
Ann: The man at the door asked us to go down to reception to speak to the manager.
N: The manager told them that they had to leave the hotel because it was overbooked. So, Ann and Jolie had to go to a different hotel and it wasn't nearly as nice as the first one. So how did these reserved and paid-for vacations go so wrong? Well, like many companies offering vacations on the Internet, Travelsoon isn't a tour operator. It's just an agent offering services from other companies. So, a vacation that looks like a complete package can be made up of lots of different arrangements involving many other companies. Each company should communicate important information to Travelsoon, and in these two situations, that didn't happen.

AUDIO AND VIDEO SCRIPTS 113

Workbook Contents

Unit

7	Leisure time	38
8	Appearance	44
9	Habits	50
10	Stories	56
11	In the news	62
12	Travel stories	68

Audio scripts 74

7 Leisure time

1 VOCABULARY

A Look at the activities below. Do you usually do them inside, outside, or both? Write **I** (inside), **O** (outside), **B** (both).

_____ 1. go horseback riding
_____ 2. catch up with friends
_____ 3. practice martial arts
_____ 4. build a website
_____ 5. go to concerts
_____ 6. go to flea markets
_____ 7. do gardening
_____ 8. have brunch

B Write the verbs from the box next to the correct activities.

have	practice	catch up
go	do	

1. _____ to flea markets, to concerts
2. _____ gardening, yoga
3. _____ with friends, on the news
4. _____ brunch, coffee with friends
5. _____ martial arts, the piano

C Circle the correct words to complete the sentences.

1. Nikki likes to do *gardening / a website* in her backyard.
2. Ted likes to go shopping at *flea markets / concerts*.
3. Jenny and Dave always catch up with *brunch / friends* on Saturdays.
4. Sally loves music but she rarely goes to *concerts / markets*.
5. Linda goes horseback *riding / practicing* several times a week.
6. Erik and Mike practice *concerts / martial arts* together.

2 LISTENING

🔊 Go to www.oxfordlearn.com. Download the audio for Unit 7.

A Listening Skill: Predicting content Look at the pictures below. What do you think these people are doing? Write your predictions.

1. _____   2. _____

3. _____   4. _____

B Listen. Check your predictions in Part A.

C Listen again. Circle the correct answers.

1. Noelle used to _____.
   a. train for the marathon   b. build websites   c. go skiing
2. Kristine used to _____.
   a. go to flea markets   b. take cooking lessons   c. go horseback riding
3. Nicholas used to _____.
   a. play soccer   b. go to concerts   c. practice martial arts
4. The two women are going to have brunch at a _____.
   a. restaurant   b. café   c. bank

UNIT 7   39

3 GRAMMAR: The present perfect continuous and the present perfect

A Use the words to write sentences with the present perfect and the present perfect continuous.

1. I / study
   I've studied _____.
   I've been studying _____.

2. he / wait
   _____.
   _____.

3. it / rain
   _____?
   _____?

4. what / you / do
   _____?
   _____?

B Complete the sentences with the present perfect.

1. I've been going to concerts.
   _____
   to three concerts this week.

2. Martin has been having cooking lessons.
   _____
   two lessons already this month.

3. Naomi and Kenji have been playing table tennis.
   _____ two games today.

4. I've been getting a lot of sleep.
   _____ for eight hours today.

C Complete the conversations with the present perfect or the present perfect continuous form of the words in parentheses.

1. A: Do you want to have lunch?
   B: Sorry. I _____ just _____ lunch with Dave. (have)

2. A: _____ the book I gave you? (you / finish)
   B: Yes. I'll give it back to you tomorrow.

3. A: What _____ lately? (she / do)
   B: _____ for a race. (train)

4. A: How many times _____ France? (you / visit)
   B: Actually, I _____ France. (never)

40

4 READING

A **Reading Skill: Scanning** Scan the text. Answer these questions.

A(n) _____ person has a score of 8.   A(n) _____ person has a score of 16.

A(n) _____ person has a score of 12.   A(n) _____ person has a score of 20.

How Active Are You?

Read the questionnaire and circle the answers about you. Then add up the numbers. Check your results at the bottom of the page.

What have you been doing lately?
1. I've been getting a lot of sleep.
2. I've been training on my own.
3. I've been taking a course.
4. I've been hanging out with friends.

How many times have you turned off your cell phone today?
1. I haven't turned it on yet!
2. I've turned it off two or three times.
3. I've turned it off more than five times.
4. I never turn off my cell phone!

What do you usually do on Friday night?
1. I go to bed early.
2. I cook dinner.
3. I cook dinner and invite friends over.
4. I go to a concert or a party.

How do you relax?
1. I watch TV.
2. I watch a movie with a friend.
3. I have brunch with friends.
4. I go to a party.

How much exercise have you gotten this week?
1. Less than one hour.
2. About an hour.
3. More than an hour.
4. Over two hours.

What's your score?
5-9: You are kind of a lazy person.
10-14: You are not lazy but not very active either.
15-19: You are very energetic.
20: You are a really active person.

B According to the questionnaire, what kind of person are you? _____

C Answer the questions about you.
1. What have you been doing lately? _____
2. What do you usually do on a Friday night? _____
3. How do you relax? _____
4. How much exercise do you get every week? _____

UNIT 7   41

5 WRITING

A Think of a person you know well. Take the quiz on page 41 again for this person and his/her life. Complete the chart below about this person.

Name: _____	
Score	**Kind of person**

B Answer the questions about this person.

1. How long have you known this person? _____
2. What has this person been doing? _____
3. What has this person done in his/her life? _____
4. What does this person do in his/her free time? _____

C Write a paragraph about the person you know and describe what kind of person he/she is. Use information from the quiz, the questions from Part B, and from what you know about him/her.

6 CULTURE TALK!
Expensive Collectibles

A Read the chart. Then answer the questions below.

What?	From when?	How much is it worth today? (U.S. dollars)
the Three Skilling Yellow stamp from Sweden	1857	$2.3 million
a GI Joe action figure from 1963	1963	$200,000
the Honus Wagner baseball card	1909	$2.8 million
the first Batman comic book	1940	$1.75 million
a gold smartphone cover by Miansai	2000 – now	$10,000

1. Which collectible is worth the most?
2. Which collectible is from 1940?
3. How much is the most expensive stamp worth? Where is it from?
4. Why does the smartphone cover by Miansai cost $10,000?
5. How much is the GI Joe action figure from 1963 worth?

B Answer the questions about you.

1. Did you ever collect anything in the past? Do you have any collectibles now?
2. Which of the things in the chart would you like to buy? Why?
3. Do you think people will stop collecting stamps in the future? Why or why not?
4. What are some other expensive collectibles?

C GO ONLINE! Research at least three expensive or unusual things that people collect.

What do they collect?	How much is it worth?	Interesting details

D Tell a partner about the collectibles you researched in Part C.

8 Appearance

1 VOCABULARY

A Are the words nouns or adjectives? Circle the correct answers.

1. bald — noun / adjective
2. confident — noun / adjective
3. beard — noun / adjective
4. neat — noun / adjective
5. studious — noun / adjective
6. scruffy — noun / adjective
7. mustache — noun / adjective
8. wavy — noun / adjective
9. clean — noun / adjective
10. messy — noun / adjective
11. shy — noun / adjective

B Complete the chart with the words from Part A.

Appearance	Personality

C Match the sentences with the correct answers.

_____ 1. When I was younger I used to have wavy hair.   a. I was very studious.

_____ 2. I was very hardworking in college.   b. I never look scruffy.

_____ 3. I am usually confident when I give a presentation.   c. Now, I'm bald.

_____ 4. I am neat and always careful of my appearance.   d. I've never had a beard.

_____ 5. I don't like any hair on my face.   e. I always practice a lot.

2 LISTENING

🔊 Go to www.oxfordlearn.com.　Download the audio for Unit 8.

A Check (✓) the words that describe the person in the picture.
- ☐ wavy hair
- ☐ scruffy
- ☐ neat
- ☐ clean
- ☐ beard
- ☐ studious
- ☐ young
- ☐ old

🔊 **B Listening Skill:** Listening for descriptive words Listen. Match the people with the descriptions.

_____ 1. Ralph   a. wavy hair, neat, and shy

_____ 2. Tim   b. wavy hair, fashionable, and confident

_____ 3. Sandra   c. black hair, studious, and scruffy

🔊 **C** Listen again. What is the other person in each conversation like? Write **T** (true) or **F** (false).

_____ 1. The other person in Conversation 1 has a beard.

_____ 2. The other person in Conversation 2 has long hair.

_____ 3. The other person in Conversation 3 isn't shy.

_____ 4. The other person in Conversation 3 looks like Sandra.

3 GRAMMAR: Used to

A Write sentences about the people in the pictures below with the affirmative or negative forms of *used to*.

Yuma

Gabriela

Jayson

B Complete the conversations. Use the words in parentheses and *use to* or *used to*.

1. A: Did you _____ in middle school? (have / short hair)

   B: No, I _____. My hair has always been long.

2. A: Where did Mark _____? (work)

   B: He _____ in a bank.

3. A: Did Maria _____ a photographer? (be)

   B: Yes, _____. Now, she's a graphic artist.

4. A: How did David _____? (look)

   B: He _____ scruffy. (be)

5. A: Did Tara _____ the piano? (play)

   B: No, she _____.

6. A: Why did you _____ your bike to school? (ride)

   B: I wanted to stay active.

C Answer the questions about you.

1. What did you use to do for fun when you were a child?

   _____

2. Did you use to wear school uniforms in school?

   _____

3. Did you use to ride your bike to school?

   _____

4. What TV shows did you use to watch when you were younger?

   _____

4 READING

A Read the article. Why does style matter in business?

From Hoodie to Suit

In the past, what people wore to work used to be very predictable. Men who worked in offices wore suits and ties, while women wore jackets and skirts. In many professions, mustaches were acceptable but beards were considered unprofessional. According to Amanda Brown, a human resources expert, workplace fashion in the 21st century is much more varied, but things haven't really changed in most workplaces.

"In start-up companies in the high tech industry, employees can pretty much wear what they like," Brown says. "Employees can be neat or scruffy. The management doesn't care. Often, this is a way that a company shows its confidence. The company is saying that they don't have to 'dress to impress.'" Yet, when these companies grow, there is often a noticeable change in what employees wear. Usually, staff members dress more conservatively.

What causes this change? "When a company grows, the employees need to interact with more people and with a variety of different people," Brown says. "Most companies still want to do business with people who are well dressed. For these companies, a neat person is a responsible person. Look at how Mark Zuckerberg looks now. He used to wear hoodies all the time, but now we see him more often in suits. Because he is running a large company, he wants to show that he's dependable."

B Answer the questions.

1. When was workplace fashion very predictable? _____
2. How is workplace fashion these days? _____
3. In what kinds of companies can workers choose what they want to wear? _____
4. Why does Mark Zuckerberg now wear suits? _____

C Write answers to these questions.

1. Do you prefer casual or more professional clothes? Why?
_____

2. Do you judge people by their appearance? Why or why not?
_____

3. What do you think your appearance says about your personality?
_____

4. If you were the boss of your own company, how would you dress? Why?
_____

UNIT 8   47

5 WRITING

A Complete the email message with the correct words.

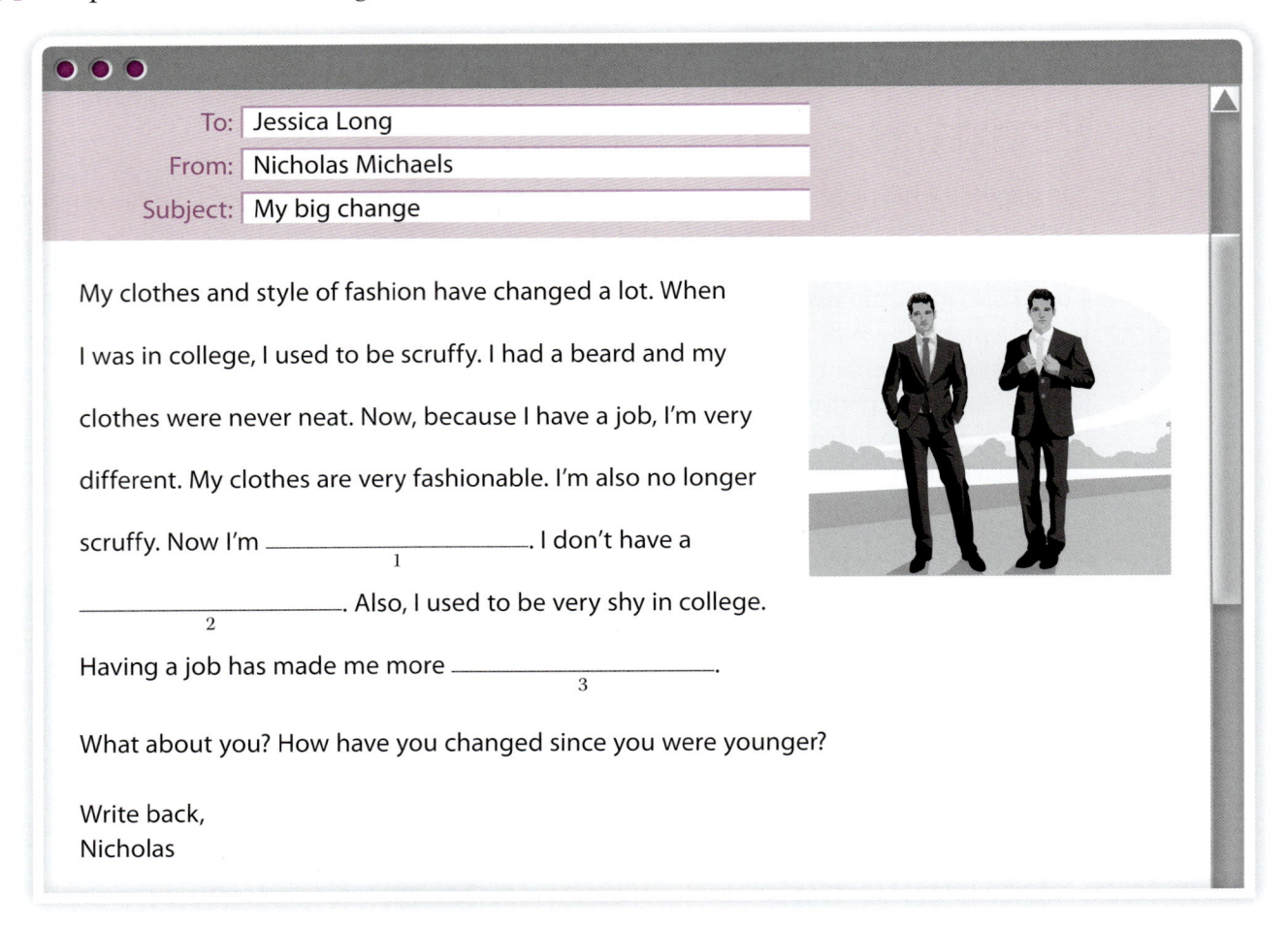

To: Jessica Long
From: Nicholas Michaels
Subject: My big change

My clothes and style of fashion have changed a lot. When I was in college, I used to be scruffy. I had a beard and my clothes were never neat. Now, because I have a job, I'm very different. My clothes are very fashionable. I'm also no longer scruffy. Now I'm _____1_____. I don't have a _____2_____. Also, I used to be very shy in college. Having a job has made me more _____3_____.

What about you? How have you changed since you were younger?

Write back,
Nicholas

B **Writing Skill:** Making a cluster diagram How have you changed in the last five years? Brainstorm ideas in the cluster diagram.

Changes
— Personality
— Appearance

Personality
Before: _____
After: _____

Appearance
Before: _____
After: _____

C Write a paragraph about how you have changed. Use your notes from Part B.

48

6 CULTURE TALK!
Makeover TV Shows

A Read the descriptions of the shows in the chart. Then write the names from the box in the correct places.

School Pride
Extreme Makeover: Home Edition
Beauty Colosseum
The Restaurant Inspector
Hotel Impossible

Name of show	Country	Description
	the U.S.	Viewers have their home completely rebuilt.
	the U.K.	A famous chef helps restaurants improve their food and service.
	the U.K.	A famous hotel expert helps hotels improve their service and design.
	Japan	Women send in videos of themselves. If they are selected, they get free plastic surgery.
	the U.S.	Students ask the show to renovate their school.

B Answer the questions about you and your culture.

1. Are there any makeover TV shows in your country? What are they about?
2. Have you watched any of these TV shows before? If not, would you watch any of them? Why or why not?
3. Do you have an idea for a makeover TV show? What would it be about?

C GO ONLINE! Research an unusual makeover TV show. Complete the chart.

Country _____

Name	Description

D Tell a partner about the TV show you researched in Part C.

UNIT 8   49

9 Habits

1 VOCABULARY

A Match the two parts of the expressions.

____ 1. catch up   a. an alarm
____ 2. go   b. my messages
____ 3. ride   c. the trash
____ 4. get up   d. to bed late
____ 5. use   e. chores
____ 6. do   f. a bike to school
____ 7. take out   g. on the news
____ 8. check   h. early

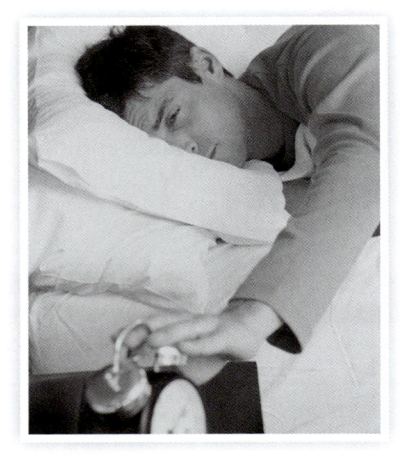

B Complete the sentences with the verbs from the box.

take out	go
do	check
use	ride

1. I _____ a bike to school when the weather is good.
2. Miles tries not to _____ to bed too late on weeknights.
3. Adam and Karina argue about who has to _____ the trash.
4. I wish I didn't have to _____ an alarm, so I can sleep until noon.
5. Our teacher gets upset when we _____ our messages in class.
6. I always _____ chores on the weekend because I'm busy during the week.

C Circle the correct words to complete the sentences.

1. Joan doesn't *use an alarm / check her messages* on Sunday mornings because she sleeps late.
2. To keep your house clean, you need to *get up early / take out the trash* regularly.
3. I go online every morning to *check up on the news / do chores*.
4. When Sue is tired, she tries to *go to bed / get up* early.
5. In order to stay active, John usually *takes out the trash / rides his bike to school*.
6. Because I have a long morning commute, I have to *catch / get* up early.

50

2 LISTENING

🔊 Go to www.oxfordlearn.com. Download the audio for Unit 9.

A How often do you do these things? Write a frequency word—*every day, always, never*—under each picture.

1. _____

2. _____

3. _____

4. _____

B Listening Skill: Listening for frequency words Listen. Match the person to the correct frequency adverb.

_____ 1. sister   a. never

_____ 2. brother   b. always

_____ 3. professor   c. usually

_____ 4. roommate   d. sometimes

C Listen again. Write **T** (true) or **F** (false).

_____ 1. Speaker 1 lives with her sister.

_____ 2. Her sister is probably a hardworking person.

_____ 3. Speaker 2's brother woke up second.

_____ 4. His brother had to finish his assignments this morning.

_____ 5. Speaker 3 said that the students were taking a test.

_____ 6. The students were using their phones that day.

_____ 7. Speaker 4's roommate doesn't like doing chores.

_____ 8. The trash is in the roommate's bedroom now.

UNIT 9   51

3 GRAMMAR: Questions with *How long*

A Complete the conversations with the correct words.

1. A: How long _____ you a member of the basketball team?
   B: I was a member for three years.
2. A: How long _____ you _____ chores?
   B: I have been doing chores for two hours.
3. A: How long _____ Frida _____ Korean?
   B: She's studied Korean for a year.
4. A: How long _____ they _____ for the race?
   B: They trained for the race for three months.

B Put the words in the correct order.

1. studied / have / you / long / how / English
   _____?
2. 2010 / a / was / Fred / from / 2013 / programmer / to
   _____.
3. you / how / living / here / long / have / been
   _____?
4. months / student / a / has / for / Maria / been / university / six
   _____.
5. how / in / long / you / New York / stay / did
   _____?
6. years / for / teacher / has / a / William / been / many
   _____.

C Answer the questions about you. Write complete sentences.

1. How long have you known your best friend?
   _____
2. How long have you studied English?
   _____
3. How long did you sleep last night?
   _____
4. How long have you been a student at this school?
   _____
   _____

4 READING

A Read the article. What does the title mean?

Unusual Homes

Most people don't like sleeping in airplanes. Some people don't mind it at all. Then there are some who want to sleep in them for their entire lives. Erik Rogers created his house using an old Boeing 727 aircraft.

How long have you been living here?
I've been living here for three years.

How long did it take to build?
It took me roughly ten years, and about three years to plan. Of course, I wasn't working on it all the time.

How do you use the original parts of the plane?
Well, the airplane has many of the features of a house. For example, it has a kitchen, bathroom, and a water tank. When I renovated the plane to fit my needs and tastes, I didn't change too much. The original kitchen is still a kitchen, for example. Of course, I had to install a shower in one of the original bathrooms, but the water comes from the original water tank.

How do you use the cockpit?
Well, I like the features of the cockpit, the steering wheels, and the control console, so I kept them. I use it as an office mainly. I have Wi-Fi and a computer in there. I go there to read, check my email, and catch up on the news.

What do you do when you're not converting airplanes?
I was an engineer for 30 years. Now, I'm a freelance writer. I've been a writer for ten years.

B Read the article again. Write **T** (true) or **F** (false). Then correct the false statements.

_____ 1. Erik has been living in this house for three years.

_____ 2. This house is made from an old Boeing 777.

_____ 3. Erik didn't change anything in the airplane.

_____ 4. Erik uses the cockpit as a bedroom.

_____ 5. Erik is a freelance writer.

C **Reading Skill: Using context clues** Use context clues to match each word with the correct meaning.

_____ 1. convert   a. where captains of airplanes sit

_____ 2. renovate   b. about, around

_____ 3. roughly   c. to make something new or to update

_____ 4. cockpit   d. to change and transform

UNIT 9   53

5 WRITING

A Complete this email from Rob Santos, who lives on a houseboat in Sausalito, CA, with the correct words from the box.

| materials | animator |
| fixer-upper | bohemian |

To: Erik Rogers
From: Rob Santos
Subject: Houseboat or airplane?

Dear Mr. Rogers,

I just read an article about your life in an airplane and it makes me want to transform a plane into a home, too. The problem is that I live on a boat now, and I don't know if I want to stay here or not.

My houseboat is in Sausalito, where I work as a full-time _____1_____. Because the job doesn't pay a lot, even though it's really fun and exciting, I wanted to live in a place that wasn't expensive. I even thought about living a cheap _____2_____ lifestyle, too. I finally bought the boat and used whatever _____3_____ I could find to renovate it.

I'm really proud of all the work I put into renovating this houseboat, but I really want to try living in an airplane, too. I just don't want to get stuck with a _____4_____ that is expensive to update.

Please write back,
Rob Santos

B Complete the chart with advantages and disadvantages of living in an airplane.

Advantages	Disadvantages

C Write a paragraph from Erik Rogers that responds to the email from Rob Santos. Use the information from the chart in Part B.

6 CULTURE TALK!
Beds Around the World

A Read the information in the chart about beds. Then answer the questions below.

Origin	Name	Description
China	kang	A *kang* is a platform bed made of bricks. You can light a fire inside the platform, so it is a very warm place to sleep.
South Korea	yo	A *yo* is a thin mattress. Traditionally, people in South Korea slept on the mattress on the floor. It's much harder than a bed. During the day, people store it in a closet.
the U.S.	murphy bed	A murphy bed is attached to a wall. During the day, it is vertical rather than horizontal. It's useful in small apartments.
Canada	snow bed	Traditionally, the Inuit people made temporary houses of snow. Inside, they made a platform of snow. They put fur on top.
Europe	trundle bed	A trundle bed has wheels and very short legs. During the day, people put it underneath another bed.

1. Which bed is probably the warmest?
2. Which bed can be put away during the day?
3. Which beds are platforms?
4. Which bed goes under another bed?
5. Which bed is the hardest?

B Answer the questions about you and your country.
1. What kind of bed do most people use in your country?
2. In your country, do people want to be warm or cool when they are in bed?
3. Which bed in the chart is the most comfortable? Why?
4. Which bed in the chart is the most interesting? Why?

C **GO ONLINE!** Research about beds in different countries. Take notes in the chart below.

Origin	Name	Description

D Tell a partner about the bed you researched in Part C.

10 Stories

1 VOCABULARY

A Match each description with the kind of story.

____ 1. These are stories about robots, the future, and other planets. a. children's literature

____ 2. You might cry when reading this kind of book. b. historical fiction

____ 3. These stories often have pictures. c. biography

____ 4. These are stories about the past. d. science fiction

____ 5. These stories are usually about cowboys and horses. e. romance

____ 6. This kind of book is about a person's life. f. western

B Write the correct kind of story.

1. Detective Jones opened the door slowly to find the lights on in the apartment, but there was no one inside. When he walked into the living room, he saw the strangest thing he'd ever seen in his life.
   _____

2. Barack Obama, the 44th president of the United States, was born in Hawaii in 1961.
   _____

3. Long before he could see it, Caecilius could hear the sound of the large crowd that had already gathered in the Colosseum. He hoped he was in time for the arrival of the gladiators.
   _____

4. Sammy was a hamster, who lived near a river. His friend William, the beaver, lived next door.
   _____

C Write the story types in the most logical places in the chart.

| science fiction | western | romance | biography |
| fantasy | children's literature | mystery | historical fiction |

For children	For adults	For both

2 LISTENING

🔊 Go to www.oxfordlearn.com. Download the audio for Unit 10.

A How much interest do you have in these books? Number them from *1* (low) to *4* (high).

B **Listening Skill:** **Asking yourself questions** Read the first lines from four different stories. Ask yourself and write down one question for each. Then listen and check if your questions are answered.

1. "Just as Officer Davis walked up to the bank, two people rushed out of the door and ran across the street."
   _____?

2. "I have something important to tell you," she said as she sat down inside the café.
   _____?

3. "Martin Cooper graduated from the Illinois Institute of Technology in 1950 and later became one of the greatest inventors in wireless communication."
   _____?

4. "The mother bird taught the scared baby bird the most important lesson in his life."
   _____?

C Listen again. Answer the questions.

1. Who did the police officer recognize?

2. Why was the man unable to speak?

3. What did Martin Cooper invent?

4. What is the baby bird learning to do?

3 GRAMMAR: Reported questions

A Check (✓) the correct sentences. Correct the incorrect sentences.

☐ 1. He said he is tired.
☐ 2. She told me she hasn't finished her work.
☐ 3. Yuki said she wasn't coming to the party.
☐ 4. Dave told me he is reading *The Lord of the Rings*.
☐ 5. She asked me if I had seen a good movie lately.
☐ 6. He asked me if do I need help with my math homework.

B Change the statements from direct speech to reported speech.

1. "I don't like going to the movies."
   She told me she _____.
2. "Class on Friday is canceled."
   The teacher said _____.
3. "I'm going to ask my girlfriend to marry me."
   He said he _____.
4. "I can't talk to you right now."
   She said she _____.
5. "Mona went to the library to study."
   She told me Mona _____.
6. "Are you reading a good book?"
   He asked _____.

C Complete the conversation with the words in parentheses.

A: Do you want to go see that new fantasy movie?

B: I thought you said you _____₁_____ fantasy movies. (hate)

A: Usually, I do. But I heard it's really good.

B: Really? Leon saw it and he said it _____₂_____ terrible. (is)

A: Well, we could always see that new science fiction film. They said it _____₃_____ based on a book. (is)

B: I'm not sure. The newspapers said the actors _____₄_____ such a good job acting. (not / do)

A: Let's just go to Mike's apartment and watch a movie there. He said he _____₅_____ a lot of good movies. (have)

58

4 READING

A Read the article. What is so special about this boy?

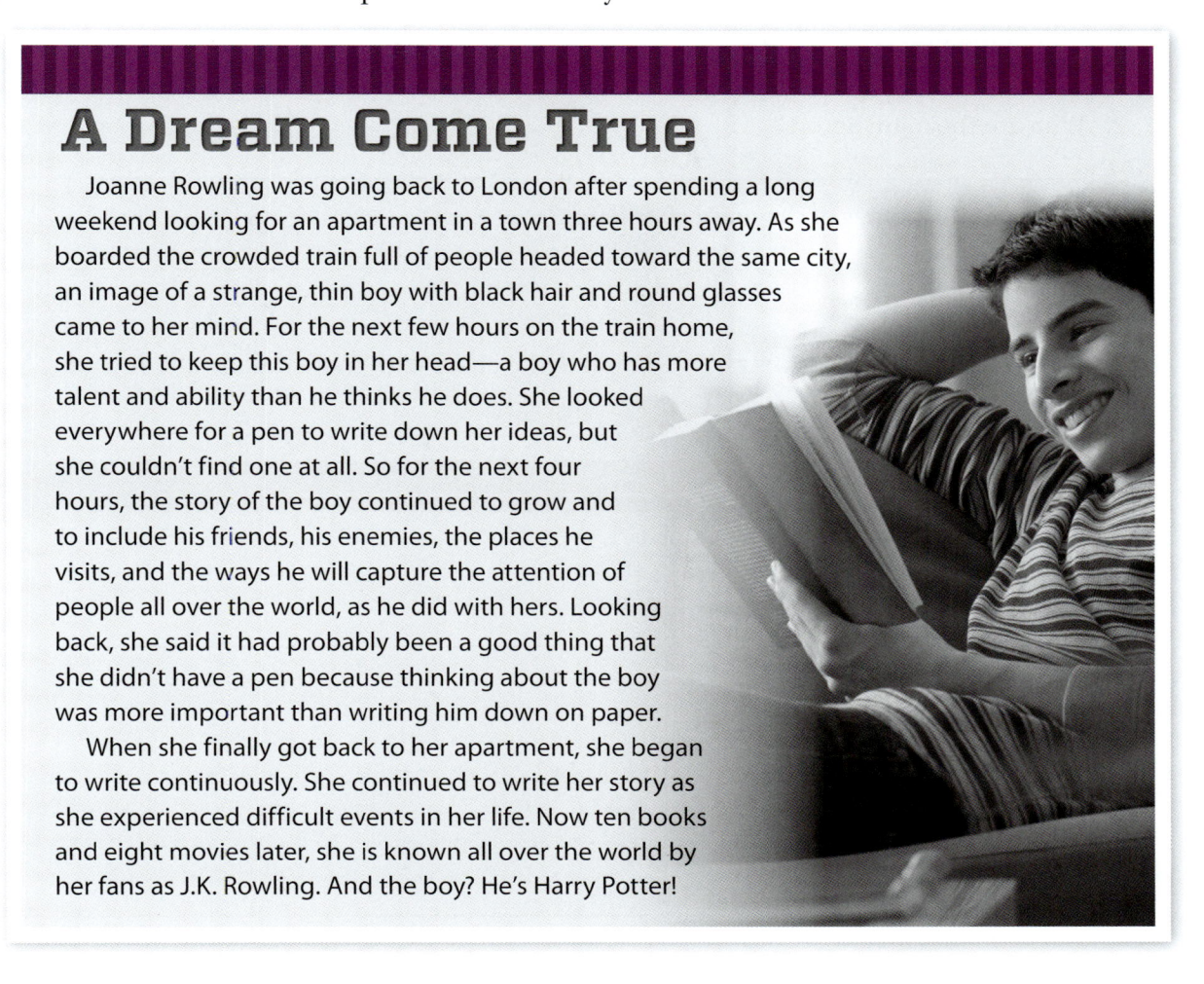

A Dream Come True

Joanne Rowling was going back to London after spending a long weekend looking for an apartment in a town three hours away. As she boarded the crowded train full of people headed toward the same city, an image of a strange, thin boy with black hair and round glasses came to her mind. For the next few hours on the train home, she tried to keep this boy in her head—a boy who has more talent and ability than he thinks he does. She looked everywhere for a pen to write down her ideas, but she couldn't find one at all. So for the next four hours, the story of the boy continued to grow and to include his friends, his enemies, the places he visits, and the ways he will capture the attention of people all over the world, as he did with hers. Looking back, she said it had probably been a good thing that she didn't have a pen because thinking about the boy was more important than writing him down on paper.

When she finally got back to her apartment, she began to write continuously. She continued to write her story as she experienced difficult events in her life. Now ten books and eight movies later, she is known all over the world by her fans as J.K. Rowling. And the boy? He's Harry Potter!

B Read the article again. Complete the sentences below.

1. Joanne was _____ when she had an idea for a fictional character.
2. She _____ to write down her ideas.
3. The character she imagined was a boy who has _____.
4. When she got home, she _____.
5. She continued to write even though _____.

C Answer the questions.

1. Why was Joanne taking a train back to London?
   _____
2. What is the personality of the boy like?
   _____
3. Why was it lucky that she couldn't find a pen?
   _____
4. Why is she famous now?
   _____

5 WRITING

A What is your favorite movie? Answer the questions below.

1. What kind of story is it?
   _____

2. Who are the main actors?
   _____

3. What are the names of the main characters?
   _____

B **Writing Skill: Summarizing** Complete the chart with more details about your favorite movie.

Title of the movie: _____	
1. What happens in the beginning of the movie?	
2. What are the five most important events that happen to the character(s)?	
3. What happens to the character(s) at the end of the movie?	

C Write a summary of the movie. Use your notes in Part B.

D Compare your summary with a partner.

60

6 CULTURE TALK!
Books and Reading

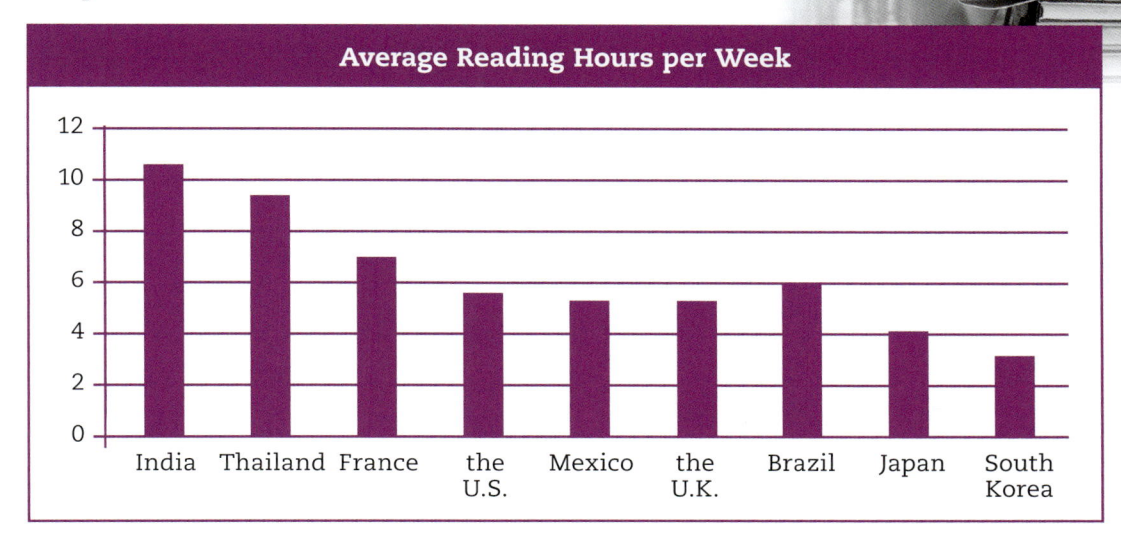

A Read the chart. Is your country on this chart? Answer the questions that follow.

Average Reading Hours per Week

- India: ~10.5
- Thailand: ~9.5
- France: ~7
- the U.S.: ~5.6
- Mexico: ~5.3
- the U.K.: ~5.3
- Brazil: ~6
- Japan: ~4
- South Korea: ~3

1. Which country reads the most? How many hours per week do people there read?
2. Which country reads the least? How many hours per week do people there read?
3. In which countries do people read on average for 5.3 hours a week?
4. Why do you think some countries read more than others?
5. What do you think people in these countries do when they're not reading?

B Answer these questions about you.
1. How many hours do you read each week? Each month?
2. Who is your favorite author?
3. What's the name of the last book you read? Did you enjoy it? Why?
4. What book would you recommend to a friend? Why?

C **GO ONLINE!** Research information about books and reading in another country. Take notes in the chart below.

Country	Hours of reading

D Tell a partner about the trends you researched in Part C.

UNIT 10

11 In the news

1 VOCABULARY

A Unscramble the letters and write the events.

1. iioxenhbti _____
2. topssr teven _____
3. rife _____
4. stationmonred _____
5. odolf _____
6. mirec _____
7. ohniasf hows _____
8. nioletec _____

B Write the correct word(s) from Part A for each sentence.

1. People vote to choose government officials. _____
2. People walk to show their concern for problems. _____
3. An event that usually involves the police. _____
4. An event that is usually held at museums. _____
5. Designers use these events to promote new clothes. _____
6. When water spreads to streets, houses, and fields. _____

C Complete the paragraph with the correct words.

   My first year as a news photographer in New York was very eventful. In my first week, I had to take pictures of a _____(1) caused by a river nearby. The cleanup afterwards took a long time. The following week, I tried to take pictures of a _____(2) caused by lightning in the forest, but it was too hot and dangerous. In February, I attended a major _____(3) between two rival baseball teams. Then a few weeks later, I got to attend a _____(4) featuring many famous clothing designers.

62

2 LISTENING

🔊 Go to www.oxfordlearn.com. Download the audio for Unit 11.

A Check (✓) the events that have happened in your area or country recently.
- ☐ an exhibition
- ☐ an election
- ☐ a flood
- ☐ a crime
- ☐ a demonstration
- ☐ a sports event

🔊 **B** **Listening Skill:** **Listening for main ideas** Listen. Check the events the speakers experienced.

1. ☐ a crime   ☐ a fire   ☐ a flood
2. ☐ a demonstration ☐ a fashion show   ☐ a sports event
3. ☐ an election   ☐ a demonstration   ☐ a fashion show
4. ☐ a crime   ☐ an election   ☐ a fire

🔊 **C** Listen again. Circle the words that you hear.

1. burnt   water   people   smoke
2. basketball   team   shouting   lost
3. vote   president   excited   council
4. police   money   bank   window

UNIT 11 63

3 GRAMMAR: *While* and *when* clauses

A Complete the sentences with *while* or *when*.

1. He was texting me _____ he was having dinner in a restaurant.
2. It started to rain _____ I was waiting for my wife outside.
3. Maria was delighted _____ her boss told her about the promotion.
4. Dave almost fell asleep _____ he was driving home from work yesterday.
5. Steve lost his wallet _____ he was traveling in Thailand.
6. Luna found a five-dollar bill _____ she was walking to work.

B Look at the pictures. Write sentences with *while* or *when*.

1. _____

2. _____

3. _____

4. _____

C Write sentences that are true for you with *while* and *when*.

1. _____
2. _____
3. _____
4. _____
5. _____
6. _____

4 READING

A Read the article. Where can you find therapy dogs?

Therapy Dogs

In the United States, travelers will often see dogs walking around airports. These aren't security dogs to stop crime; they are "therapy dogs." They wear special vests that say "Pet Me!" People who are stressed and anxious about traveling can interact and touch the dogs. Scientists and psychologists say that dogs in general provide many mental and health benefits to people because they provide stress relief.

It's not just travelers who are afraid of flying or have never flown who pet the dogs. Many other people do as well. Heidi Huebner, director of volunteer dogs at Los Angeles International Airport, said, "While some people are worrying about being late for their flight, others are relaxing and having fun with the dogs. People start smiling and talking to each other. As a result, you can feel the stress levels drop."

Five-year-old Carina McCaskill was low on energy and tired because she and her family were flying back to Los Angeles from Brazil after a sports event. She quickly became happy when she saw a therapy dog. Carina later sent a video. "Thank you for visiting us at the airport so I would be happy," she said in the video. Now Carina wants to go back and see the dog again.

B **Reading Skill:** Identifying cause and effect (2) Complete the chart with the correct causes and effects. Then underline the words that tell you in the article.

Cause	Effect
Dogs provide stress relief.	
	You can feel the stress levels drop.
	Carina McCaskill was tired.
Carina saw a therapy dog.	

C Answer the questions with information about you.

1. Do you think having therapy dogs in airports is a good idea? Why or why not?
   _____

2. What kind of people do you think might not like therapy dogs in the airport?
   _____

3. Do you think therapy dogs should be allowed to fly in airplanes to help people relax? Why or why not?
   _____

4. How else can people who are afraid of flying feel more relaxed and calm?
   _____

5 WRITING

A Complete the comments below with the correct words from the box.

| away | about | with | at | to | around |

Home | **News** | **Business** | **Sports** | **Entertainment** | **Blog** | **Chat**

ELLEN JACOB

I just saw the cutest therapy dogs at Los Angeles International Airport! What do you think of therapy dogs?

AMY: I think they're great! I have a five-year-old son who always misses our dog, Molly, while we're traveling. Now he can interact and play _____(1) dogs like Molly. This makes him worry less _____(2) leaving Molly at home.

SIMON: I don't know about this. My twin daughters really don't like dogs, and they're slightly allergic _____(3) them. I'm afraid my daughters will run _____(4) and start crying if they see these dogs walking towards them.

KATHRYN: I don't think we need more dogs or people at the airport. If I'm running and rushing to catch my flight, I don't want to have to worry about walking _____(5) them and the people petting them.

VICKY: I prefer having cats _____(6) the airport. Dogs have too much energy and bark at you. Cats, on the other hand, are calmer and less scary.

B What are the people's opinions of therapy dogs? Complete the chart below.

Name	Agree or disagree?	Why?
Amy		
Simon		
Kathryn		
Vicky		

C Write your own comment with your opinion of therapy dogs at the airport. You can use information from the chart or your own ideas.

6 CULTURE TALK!
Being Fired for Lateness

A Read the information in the chart. Then answer the questions below.

Country	Percent of employers who have fired a worker for lateness
India	42
Brazil	26
France	22
the U.K.	21
China	20

1. Which country has the highest percentage of employers firing people for lateness?
2. Which country has the lowest percentage of employers firing people for lateness?
3. Why do you think so many employers in India fire people for being late?
4. Do you think your country has a high or low percentage of employers who fire people for lateness? Why?

B Answer the questions about you and your culture.
1. Are people usually late or on time in your culture?
2. Are you often late for class or meeting friends? Why or why not?
3. Describe a time you were late and other people were upset with you. What happened?
4. Why do different cultures have different attitudes towards lateness?

C **GO ONLINE!** Research attitudes to lateness in a different country or culture. Take notes in the chart below.

Country	Attitude to lateness

D Tell a partner about the culture you researched in Part C.

UNIT 11

12 Travel stories

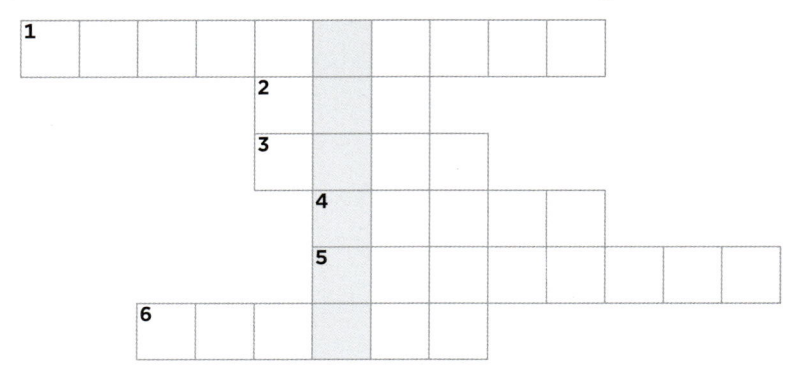

1 VOCABULARY

A Read the clues. Then write the answers in the puzzle.

1. Ask someone for these when you get lost.
2. If you're hungry, you should do this with the local food.
3. You do this when you want room service.
4. This word means to go to and spend time in a place.
5. You'll need to do this with your money if you visit a foreign country.
6. If you lose this, you'll lose your money and credit cards, too.

What is the hidden word in gray? _____

B Complete the sentences with the correct words and phrases from Part A.

1. I prefer to eat in my hotel room. I often _____ room service.
2. I love exploring different foods. When I travel, I always visit a _____ restaurant.
3. The driver doesn't know whether to turn right or left. He should ask for _____.
4. Local banks sometimes let travelers _____ currency before they travel.
5. One of my worst fears while traveling abroad is to lose my _____.
6. I heard that Florence, Italy, has some great museums. I want to _____ the city this summer.

C Complete the sentences with the correct forms of the verbs from the box.

| miss | try | call | exchange | ask |

1. I always _____ currency at the airport when I arrive in a foreign country.
2. My husband never _____ for directions when he gets lost.
3. When we _____ our flight, we had to wait for hours at the airport until the next one.
4. If you don't want to eat in a restaurant, _____ room service.
5. When I traveled a lot for business, I loved _____ the local food of the places I visited.

2 LISTENING

🔊 Go to www.oxfordlearn.com.   Download the audio for Unit 12.

A Which situation do you think is the most serious? Rank the situations from *1* (low) to *4* (high).

B Listen. Circle the correct situations.

1. lost a wallet   lost a credit card   asked for directions
2. missed a flight   got sick   asked for directions
3. asked for directions   lost a credit card   missed a flight
4. lost a wallet   asked for directions   missed a flight

C Listening Skill: Listening for key words Listen again. Match each speaker to the people that helped solve the problem.

_____ Speaker 1   a. the airline clerk
_____ Speaker 2   b. a police officer
_____ Speaker 3   c. the locals
_____ Speaker 4   d. the hotel manager

UNIT 12   69

3 GRAMMAR: Present perfect for experiences

A Circle the correct answers to complete the sentences.

1. _____ to India, but I'd like to go there sometime.
   a. I've been   b. I've never   c. I've never been
2. _____ surfing.
   a. I am never   b. I've never   c. I haven't been
3. Have you ever _____ sushi?
   a. had   b. has   c. have
4. _____ alone before.
   a. I've traveled   b. I've ever traveled   c. I've never travel
5. What's the most interesting class _____?
   a. you take   b. you've ever taken   c. you taking
6. How many times _____ abroad?
   a. are you been   b. have you ever   c. have you been
7. I've lost my wallet but _____ my passport.
   a. I never lost   b. I've ever lost   c. I've never lost

B Complete the conversations.

1. A: _____ to Brazil?
   B: Yes, I have. I was there last year.
2. A: _____?
   B: The most interesting place I've visited is the British Museum.
3. A: _____ bibimbap?
   B: Yes, I have. I had it in a South Korean restaurant. It was delicious!
4. A: Have you _____ the new Liam Hemsworth movie?
   B: No, I haven't. Who is he?

C Answer the questions with information about you.

1. Have you ever lost your cell phone?
   _____
2. What's the best book you've read?
   _____
3. How many times have you seen your favorite movie?
   _____
4. Have you ever fallen asleep at work or school?
   _____
5. Who's the most interesting person you've ever met?
   _____
6. Have you ever broken a bone?
   _____

4 READING

A Read the article. What countries are mentioned?

Frequent Flyer Mishaps

For many, the experience of traveling can become a nightmare. Passengers can encounter all kinds of difficulties en route. Here are some of the most frequent ones.

THE AIRLINE LOSES YOUR LUGGAGE Many travelers are concerned about theft or losing their passports while traveling. What's much more likely, however, is that they will lose their luggage. In the United States, airlines lose or misplace about 1% of checked luggage. As a result, passengers arrive at vacation destinations without their clothes and toiletries. Although the majority of travelers are compensated, it is typically long after the vacation is over.

YOU BOOK A SUBSTANDARD HOTEL Most people nowadays book hotels online. A result is that there are more complaints about hotels. Travelers make decisions based on descriptions of hotels on websites. Often, when people arrive at the hotel, they find that it is completely different than the one portrayed online. The Netherlands, by the way, has some of the worst budget hotels in the world.

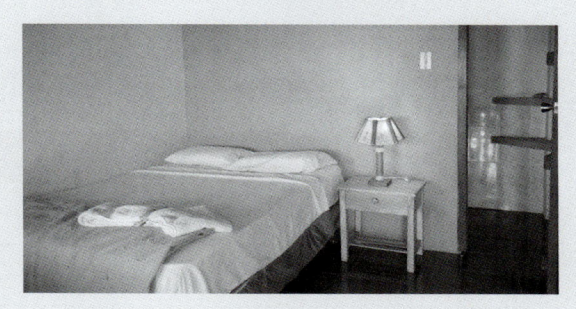

YOU MISS YOUR FLIGHT Only 0.2% of passengers who check in miss their flights. The problem is with connecting flights. In Europe, almost 5% of passengers miss their connecting flight because of delays. This can cause major problems for them, as many flights are full and it can be difficult for them to get a later flight.

B Read the article again. Write **T** (true) or **F** (false). Then correct the false statements.

_____ 1. More passengers lose their wallets than their luggage.

_____ 2. The airlines lose about 1% of checked luggage.

_____ 3. Nowadays, most people use a travel agent to book a hotel.

_____ 4. The Netherlands has some terrible budget hotels.

_____ 5. If you miss a connecting fight, you can have problems getting another flight.

C Answer the questions about you.

1. What's the worst thing that happened to you on vacation?
   _____

2. What was the worst experience you had in a hotel?
   _____

3. Would you prefer to save money by staying at a terrible hotel?
   _____

4. What was your last vacation? Where did you go?
   _____

5 WRITING

A Look at the events below. Put them in logical order from *1–6*.

___ sleep overnight at the airport

___ spend 40 minutes at the check-in counter

___ arrive at the destination

___ catch a flight

___ relax at the hotel pool

___ miss a flight

B Complete the chart with information and details from Part A. Create a story in the past.

What happened?	Details
1. missed a flight	forgot to use an alarm clock
2.	
3.	
4.	
5.	
6.	

C Write a paragraph using your ideas from Part B.

D **Writing Skill:** Self-assessing Read the paragraph you wrote in Part C. Can you find any grammar or spelling mistakes? Correct them.

6 CULTURE TALK!
Future Travel Trends

A Read the descriptions of future travel trends. Then write the names from the box in the correct places in the chart.

| Senior travel | Staycation | Bleisure | Eco-volunteering |

_____
This word means a combination of business and leisure. In the future, more people are expected to take vacation days when they travel abroad for business. This can save someone a lot of money.

_____
Because of the aging population in Europe, North America, and Asia, people can expect to see more and more luxury cruises. Ships are ideal vacation locations for senior citizens.

_____
As more people become aware of the environment, there will be more vacations where tourists participate in helping the environment. For example, visitors can plant grass on Hawaiian beaches to protect them from erosion.

_____
This word means vacationing while staying at home. Why will this be a big trend in the future? It's the best kind of vacation for the environment, and it's a great way to save money.

B Answer the questions.
1. Which vacations are best for saving money?
2. Which vacations are best for the environment?
3. Which vacation looks the best to you? Why?
4. When planning a vacation, what's the most important thing for you?

C GO ONLINE! Research future travel trends. Take notes in the chart below.

Trend	Details

D Tell a partner about the trends you researched in Part C.

UNIT 12

AUDIO SCRIPTS

Unit 7
LISTENING page 39

Conversation 1
A: Noelle! Are you still training for the marathon?
B: No, actually, I injured my leg.
A: So what are you doing for fun?
B: Well, actually, I've been taking a computer course. I'm building my own website.
A: That's fantastic. Maybe you can build one for me.

Conversation 2
A: Hey, Kristine. Have you gone horseback riding lately?
B: No. I've been going to flea markets. I have a new hobby. Antiquing. You know, buying and selling antiques.
A: Do you know anything about antiques?
B: Actually, I'm taking a course.
A: There's a course in antiques?
B: Yes, it's called Understanding Antiques.

Conversation 3
A: Hey, Nicholas. Are you still playing soccer?
B: No, I gave that up. I've been taking a martial arts course instead.
A: Kung Fu?
B: No. Tae Kwan Do.

Conversation 4
A: What are you doing next Saturday? We really need to catch up.
B: We do. How about Chinese brunch at the restaurant on Bank Street? I think it's called *dim sum*.
A: I don't really know how to use chopsticks. Plus, I don't have a lot of time that Saturday afternoon.
B: OK, no problem. We'll just grab something quick at the café on the corner.

Unit 8
LISTENING page 45

Conversation 1
A: Who's that?
B: That's Ralph.
A: That's not Ralph. That person has a beard. And he's bald. Ralph doesn't have a beard, and he's not bald. He has black hair. And Ralph's kind of scruffy. You know, the studious, academic type.

Conversation 2
A: Is that Tim over there?
B: Tim from our Economics class? No, I don't think so. That man has short hair. Tim has wavy hair and Tim is always neat, never messy. That man is a bit scruffy and serious looking. Nothing like Tim. And Tim never dances at parties. He's really shy.

Conversation 3
A: Is that your sister Sandra?
B: Who? That girl? She does look a bit like her. But that woman looks really shy. Sandra has wavy hair and she's much more fashionable. Sandra is really confident. She isn't shy at all.

Unit 9
LISTENING page 51

Speaker 1
I came home yesterday, thinking the apartment was going to be dirty and smelly. Instead, I see my sister doing chores and cleaning up the place. How surprising since she never does chores.

Speaker 2
I barely got any sleep because my brother's alarm woke me up at a quarter to five. He sometimes uses an alarm if he has to finish his assignments before class, but I wish he hadn't this morning because now I'm sleepy.

Speaker 3
Our professor usually tells us to turn off our phones and he doesn't like it when he sees us using them in class. But today we had to remind him because we caught him checking his messages while we were taking a test.

Speaker 4
My roommate doesn't help out around the house at all and always has an excuse for everything. Last night I kindly asked him if he could take out the trash. He said he wasn't feeling too well and had to go to bed early. It's so frustrating! Maybe I'll just leave the trash in his bedroom and see if he'll take it out then.

Unit 10
LISTENING page 57

1. Just as Officer Davis walked up to the bank, two people rushed out of the door and ran across the street. Officer Davis screamed at them to stop, but they simply ignored him and everyone they bumped into. The two people threw their heavy bags into a car and Officer Davis started to chase after them. He stopped immediately when he saw one of the robbers take off her mask. Officer Davis soon realized that she was not only a robber, but also his daughter.

2. "I have something important to tell you," she said as she sat down inside the café. "I hope it's good news," he joked. His smile quickly disappeared as he saw how serious her eyes looked. "I'm leaving tomorrow to go back to California so I can take over my family's business. I'm sorry, but I don't think I can see you anymore." He sat silently looking at her, unable to speak, while the rain continued to fall softly outside.

3. Martin Cooper graduated from Illinois Institute of Technology in 1950 and later became one of the greatest inventors in wireless communication. Twenty years later, Cooper came up with an idea for the first portable cellular phone while working at Motorola, Inc. This first phone weighed in at 2.5 pounds, was 10 inches long, and had a battery life of only 20 minutes. Cooper continued to work at

Motorola for 29 years, and during that time he helped to create many other inventions in mobile technology.

4. The mother bird taught the scared baby bird the most important lesson in his life. "You have to take chances and learn how to fly. You can't be so scared because you will definitely fall," said the mother. With these words, the baby bird walked to the edge of the mountain, closed his eyes, and spread his wings proudly as he jumped off.

Unit 11
LISTENING page 63

Speaker 1
I thought they'd still be closed after that incident last month, but they seemed to be open for business when I walked by the other day. The owners of the restaurant told me it started in the kitchen overnight when there weren't any customers around. Thankfully, no one got hurt and only a few things in the kitchen were damaged and burnt, including the walls that suffered minor smoke damage.

Speaker 2
I really didn't enjoy it. First of all, there were too many people. It was really crowded everywhere. And it was so noisy. Almost everyone seemed to be shouting. And on top of that, my team didn't win! The final score was three to one.

Speaker 3
All my friends were cheering for me. Even some of the teachers looked happy. Actually, I couldn't believe it. Although I'd worked hard, I didn't expect it. But I won! I'll be president of the student council for a year.

Speaker 4
The first thing I saw was a crowd of people standing around. There were several police officers there, too. Like everyone else, I was curious so I walked over to see what happened. The store window was completely broken. You could see that a lot of the items inside were stolen. A couple of police officers were walking around inside. It was just like what you see on TV.

Unit 12
LISTENING page 69

Speaker 1
I ran into a few problems when I was in São Paulo. But the most serious one was when I lost my wallet. I couldn't believe it! I spoke to the hotel manager, who was so helpful, and he called the restaurant where we had breakfast. He looked everywhere, but luckily someone found my wallet by the pool. I was so relieved.

Speaker 2
When I went to visit my cousin, I had some local food at a small market. Everything looked and tasted delicious, but after a few minutes I started to feel sick. I think it was the crab, and I'm allergic to it. I had to sit down on a bench. A police officer noticed and she came over to me. She was nice enough to drive me to the hospital.

Speaker 3
Last year, on my way to the airport to Japan, the taxi broke down and I missed my flight. I was so upset, because I had been saving up for this trip for an entire year. When I got to the check-in counter, I started to cry. Thankfully, the airline clerk calmed me down and put me on the next flight.

Speaker 4
I went to a huge market in Thailand for some shopping, you know, the typical souvenirs you buy for friends and family back home. There were so many interesting shops and stalls that I lost track of time and I got lost. I couldn't find my way out. Fortunately, the locals there told me how to get out after I asked for directions.

OXFORD
UNIVERSITY PRESS

198 Madison Avenue
New York, NY 10016 USA

Great Clarendon Street, Oxford, OX2 6DP, United Kingdom

Oxford University Press is a department of the University of Oxford.
It furthers the University's objective of excellence in research, scholarship,
and education by publishing worldwide. Oxford is a registered trade
mark of Oxford University Press in the UK and in certain other countries

© Oxford University Press 2014

The moral rights of the author have been asserted

First published in 2014

2018 2017 2016 2015 2014
10 9 8 7 6 5 4 3 2 1

No unauthorized photocopying

All rights reserved. No part of this publication may be reproduced, stored in a retrieval system, or transmitted, in any form or by any means, without the prior permission in writing of Oxford University Press, or as expressly permitted by law, by licence or under terms agreed with the appropriate reprographics rights organization. Enquiries concerning reproduction outside the scope of the above should be sent to the ELT Rights Department, Oxford University Press, at the address above

You must not circulate this work in any other form and you must impose this same condition on any acquirer

Links to third party websites are provided by Oxford in good faith and for information only. Oxford disclaims any responsibility for the materials contained in any third party website referenced in this work

Director, ELT New York: Laura Pearson
Executive Publishing Manager: Erik Gundersen
Publisher, Adult Coursebooks: Louisa van Houten
Managing Editor: Tracey Gibbins
Senior Development Editor: Cristina Zurawski
Associate Editor: Harvey Chan
Executive Art and Design Manager: Maj-Britt Hagsted
Content Production Manager: Julie Armstrong
Image Manager: Trisha Masterson
Production Coordinator: Brad Tucker

ISBN: 978 0 19 460322 5 STUDENT BOOK (PACK COMPONENT)
ISBN: 978 0 19 460334 8 STUDENT BOOK (PACK)
ISBN: 978 0 19 460370 6 ONLINE PRACTICE (PACK COMPONENT)

Printed in China

This book is printed on paper from certified and well-managed sources

STUDENT BOOK PAGES ACKNOWLEDGEMENTS

Illustrations by: Debbie Lofaso, Cover Illustration; 5W Infographics, pg. 6, 12, 18, 32, 38, 66, 78, 100, 103; Joe Taylor. pg. 22, 24, 48, 50, 51, 62, 88.

We would also like to thank the following for permission to reproduce the following photographs: "Tip" presenters used throughout the book: Yuri Arcurs/Alamy; MANDY GODBEHEAR /Alamy; Jacob Yuri Wackerhausen /Tetra Images/Corbis; violetblue /shutterstock.com. **Interior**, Andresr / shutterstock, pg. ii; Thomas Barwick/Getty Images, pg. 2; Corbis, pg. 2; Laara Cerman/Leigh Righton/Getty Images, pg. 2; Michael DeLeo/Getty Images. pg. 2; Aurora Photos / Alamy, pg. 2; redbrickstock.com / Alamy, pg. 2; Blaine Harrington III / Alamy, pg. 2; Jordan Siemens/Corbis, pg. 2; Topic Photo Agency/Corbis, pg. 3; Aurora Photos / Alamy, pg. 4; Thomas Barwick/Getty Images, pg. 4; Jordan Siemens/Corbis, pg. 4; Corbis, pg. 4; Andres Rodriguez / Alamy, pg. 4; Laara Cerman/Leigh Righton/Getty Images, pg. 4; Brandon Tabiolo/Design Pics/Corbis, pg. 4; Purestock/Getty Images, pg. 5; Mango Productions/Corbis, pg. 5; Emmanuel R Lacoste/shutterstock, pg. 5; Brooke Slezak/Getty Images, pg. 7; INSADCO Photography / Alamy, pg. 8; Hector Mandel/Getty Images, pg. 8; david pearson / Alamy, pg. 8; Presselect / Alamy, pg. 8; The Asahi Shimbun via Getty Images, pg. 8; Wavebreak Media ltd / Alamy, pg. 8; Buccina Studios/Getty Images, pg. 8; Nikola Miljkovic/Getty Images, pg. 8; Darren Kemper/Corbis, pg. 9; Nikola Miljkovic/Getty Images, pg. 10; Aurora Photos / Alamy, pg. 10; Presselect / Alamy, pg. 10; Wavebreak Media ltd / Alamy, pg. 10; MARK RALSTON/AFP/Getty Images, pg. 10; Jordan Siemens/Corbis, pg. 10; The Asahi Shimbun via Getty Images, pg.10; Tony Tremblay/Getty Images, pg. 11; Raquel Lonas/Getty Images, pg. 13; Juniors Bildarchiv GmbH / Alamy, pg. 14; Imaginechina/Corbis, pg. 14; David Marsden/Getty Images, pg. 14; Ivan Danik / Alamy, pg. 14; Blend Images / Alamy, pg. 14; Yuri/Getty Images, pg. 14; Dougal Waters/Getty Images, pg. 14; Paul Souders/Corbis, pg. 14; 4FR/Getty Images, pg. 15; Imaginechina/Corbis, pg. 16; Blend Images / Alamy, pg. 16; Ivan Danik / Alamy, pg. 16; Juniors Bildarchiv GmbH / Alamy, pg. 16; David Marsden/Getty Images, pg. 16; KidStock/Getty Images, pg. 16; Yuri/Getty Images, pg. 16; Monkey Business Images/shutterstock, pg. 17; iconics/a.collectionRF / Getty Images, pg. 19; Kevork Djansezian/Getty Images, pg. 21; Rene Frederick/Getty Images, pg. 23; stocknroll/Getty Images, pg. 25; Topic Photo Agency/Corbis, pg. 26; Sven Hagolani/Corbis, pg. 27; Wavebreak Media LTD/Wavebreak Media Ltd./Corbis, pg. 28; moodboard/Getty Images, pg. 28; Peter Kirillov/shutterstock, pg. 28; Harry Hu / Shutterstock.com, pg. 28; David Pirvu / Alamy, pg. 28; Peter M. Fisher/Corbis, pg. 28; Knauer/Johnston/Getty Images, pg. 28; Clerkenwell/Getty Images, pg. 28; Hero Images/Hero Images/Corbis, pg. 29; Wavebreak Media LTD/Wavebreak Media Ltd./Corbis, pg. 30; Clerkenwell/Getty Images, pg. 30; Andresr/shutterstock, pg. 30; Harry Hu / Shutterstock.com, pg. 30; Kali Nine LLC/Getty Images, pg. 30; Morton Beebe/Corbis, pg. 30; i love images/Getty Images, pg. 30; Flip Nicklin/Minden Pictures, pg. 31; JOHANNES EISELE/AFP/Getty Images, pg. 33; Maridav/shutterstock, pg. 34; Glow Images/Getty Images, pg. 34; Hero Images/Getty Images, pg. 34; bikeriderlondon/shutterstock, pg. 34; Cavan Images/Getty Images, pg. 34; Chad Slattery/Getty Images, pg. 34; Peter Dazeley/Getty Images, pg. 34; Hybrid Images/Getty Images, pg. 34; Hiya Images/Corbis, pg. 35; Hybrid Images/Getty Images, pg. 36; Cavan Images/Getty Images, pg. 36; Maridav/shutterstock, pg. 36; Adam Gault/Getty Images, pg. 36; redbrickstock.com / Alamy, pg. 36; Laara Cerman/Leigh Righton/Getty Images, pg. 36; Thomas Barwick/Getty Images, pg. 36; Vismar Ravagnani/Getty Images, pg. 37; Sam Edwards/Getty Images, pg. 39; Pressmaster/shutterstock, pg. 41; Chuck Eckert / Alamy, pg. 42; Samo Trebizan/shutterstock, pg. 42; Liane Cary/Getty Images, pg. 42; MBI / Alamy, pg. 42; Michael Dwyer / Alamy, pg. 42; Blend Images / Alamy, pg. 42; Westend61/Getty Images, pg. 42; Betsie Van der Meer/Getty Images, pg. 42; Ocean/Corbis, pg. 43; Westend61/Getty Images, pg. 44; Peter Dazeley/Getty Images, pg. 44; MBI / Alamy, pg. 44; Chuck Eckert / Alamy, pg. 44; Michael Dwyer / Alamy, pg. 44; Ogphoto/Getty Images, pg. 44; Liane Cary/Getty Images, pg. 44; Samo Trebizan/shutterstock, pg. 44; Wonwoo Lee/Getty Images, pg. 45; Bartlomiej Magierowski / Alamy, pg. 46; Ivan Bajic/Getty Images, pg. 47; Doug Pensinger/Getty Images, pg. 47; Betsie Van der Meer/Getty Images, pg. 47; Ocean/Corbis, pg. 47; damircudic/Getty Images, pg. 49; PS1/ZOB WENN Photos/Newscom, pg. 52; Jaren Jai Wicklund/shutterstock, pg. 53; Radius Images/Corbis, pg. 54; David Young-Wolff / Alamy, pg. 54; Cultura RM / Alamy, pg. 54; Skip Brown/Getty Image, pg. 54; YinYang/Getty Images, pg. 54; Ocean/Corbis, pg. 54; Ryan Smith/Somos Images/Corbis, pg. 54; Fuse/Getty Images, pg. 54; Tetra Images/Corbis, pg. 55; Fuse/Getty Images, pg. 56; Liane Cary/Getty Images, pg. 56; Pius Lee / Shutterstock.com, pg. 56; Skip Brown/Getty Image, pg. 56; YinYang/Getty Images, pg. 56; Cultura RM / Alamy, pg. 56; Ocean/Corbis, pg. 56; Georgianna Lane/Garden Photo World/Corbis, pg. 57; MIKE SEGAR/Reuters/Corbis, pg. 58; Jordan Siemens/Getty Images, pg. 59; KC Slagle/shutterstock, pg. 61; Regine Mahaux/Getty Images, pg. 63; zhang bo/Getty Images, pg. 64; Vivek Sharma/Getty Images, pg. 64; Laurence Mouton/Getty Images, pg. 64; Directphoto.org / Alamy, pg. 64; Thinkstock/Getty Images, pg. 64; Ryan McVay/Getty Images, pg. 64; Yeko Photo Studio/shuttertsock, pg. 64; Harald Sund/Getty Images, pg. 65; FOX 2000 PICTURES/DUNE ENTERTAINMENT/INGENIOUS MEDIA/HAISHANG FILMS / THE KOBAL COLLECTION, pg. 67; Philip Wallick/Corbis, pg. 68; Jim Kidd / Alamy, pg. 68; Monty Rakusen/Getty Images, pg. 68; Echo/Getty Images, pg. 68; IS_ImageSource/Istock, pg. 68; Alex Livesey/Getty Images, pg. 68; Caro / Alamy, pg. 68; Tetra Images/Corbis, pg. 68; Alan Copson/Getty Images, pg. 69; PhotoTalk/Getty Images, pg. 70; Tetra Images/Corbis, pg. 70; Simon Battensby/Getty Images, pg. 70; OUP/Blend Images, pg. 70; Ian Shaw / Alamy, pg. 70; Cultura RM / Alamy, pg. 70; Chuck Eckert / Alamy, pg. 70; Michael Dwyer / Alamy, pg. 70; Splash News/Newscom, pg. 71; altrendo images/Getty Images, pg. 72; epa european pressphoto agency b.v. / Alamy, pg. 73; udra11/shutterstock, pg. 74; J.A. Bracchi/Getty Images, pg. 74; Hero Images/Corbis, pg. 74; Yellow Dog Productions/Getty Images, pg. 74; Patti McConville/Getty Images, pg. 74; Martin Moxter/age footstock, pg. 74; Dave and Les Jacobs/Getty Images, pg. 74; Andrejs Zemdega/Getty Images, pg. 74; OUP/Photodisc, pg. 75; Patti McConville/Getty Images, pg. 76; Yellow Dog Productions/Getty Images, pg. 76; Hector Mandel/Getty Images, pg. 76; udra11/shutterstock, pg. 76; Hero Images/Corbis, pg. 76; Dave and Les Jacobs/Getty Images, pg. 76; J.A. Bracchi/Getty Images, pg. 76; Andrejs Zemdega/Getty Images, pg. 76; Julian Elliott Ethereal Light/Getty Images, pg. 77; Blaine Harrington III / Alamy, pg. 79; Dirk Herzog/shutterstock, pg. 81; eurobanks/shutterstock, pg. 94; wong sze yuen/shutterstock, pg. 94; Kevin Dodge/Corbis, pg. 95; OUP/Stockbyte, pg. 95; eurobanks/shutterstock, pg. 97; wong sze yuen/shutterstock, pg. 97; Kevin Dodge/Corbis, pg. 98; OUP/Stockbyte, pg. 98.

WORKBOOK PAGES ACKNOWLEDGEMENTS

Illustrations by: Debbie Lofaso, Cover Illustration; Joe Taylor, pg. 21, 22, 44, 46, 48, 57, 58.

We would also like to thank the following for permission to reproduce the following photographs: Interior, © Corbis, pg. 2; redbrickstock.com / Alamy, pg. 3, Jordan Siemens/Corbis, pg. 3, Laara Cerman/Leigh Righton/Getty Images, pg. 3; Aurora Photos / Alamy, pg. 5, Image by © Matthias Ritzmann/Corbis, pg. 5, Yafang/Shutterstock, pg. 5, Julien Tromeur/Shutterstock, pg. 5; Nejron Photo/Shutterstock, pg. 6; mama_mia/Shutterstock, pg. 7; Tdway/Shutterstock, pg. 8; Buccina Studios/Getty Images, pg. 9, Wavebreak Media ltd / Alamy, pg. 9, INSADCO Photography / Alamy, pg. 9, Image by © Randy Faris/Corbis, pg. 9; david pearson / Alamy, pg. 10; © Marla Brose/ZUMA Press/Corbis, pg. 11; © Tim Clayton/TIM CLAYTON/Corbis, pg. 12; Pete Titmuss/Alamy, pg. 13; © ArtMarie/iStock, pg. 14; Dougal Waters/Getty Images, pg. 15, Ivan Danik / Alamy, pg. 15, Yuri/Getty Images, pg. 15, Blend Images / Alamy, pg. 15; Imaginechina/Corbis, pg. 16; MIXA/Alamy, pg. 17; © Lane Oatey/Blue Jean Images/Corbis, pg. 18; Associated Press, pg. 19; Blend Images/Alamy, pg. 20; © Ocean/Corbis, pg. 23; cozyta/Shutterstock, pg. 24; Konstantin Chagin/Shutterstock, pg. 25; AntonioDiaz/Shutterstock, pg. 26; David Pirvu / Alamy, pg. 27, Clerkenwell/Getty Images, pg. 27, Harry Hu / Shutterstock.com, pg. 27; © YinYang/iStock, pg. 28, moodboard/Getty Images, pg. 28; © Dan Barnes/iStock, pg. 29; © Armando Gallo /Retna Ltd./Corbis, pg. 30; Getty Images/AFP collection, pg. 31; © Inmagine Asia/Corbis, pg. 32, Monkey Business Images/Shutterstock, pg. 32; Peter Dazeley/Getty Images, pg. 33, bikeriderlondon/shutterstock, pg. 33, Hybrid Images/Getty Images, pg. 33; Cavan Images/Getty Images, pg. 34, Maridav/shutterstock, pg. 34; © Zou Zheng/Xinhua Press/Corbis, pg. 35; © Alan Schein Photography/Corbis, pg. 36; © beckybagdanoff/iStock, pg. 37; Chuck Eckert / Alamy, pg. 38; © Hero Images/Hero Images/Corbis, pg. 39, Kucher Serhii/Shutterstock, pg. 39, Ocean/Corbis, pg. 39, Betsie Van der Meer/Getty Images, pg. 39; Michael Dwyer / Alamy, pg. 40; © Wavebreak Media Ltd./Corbis, pg. 41; Maridav/shutterstock, pg. 42, Stockbroker/Alamy, pg. 42; © Kit Kittle/CORBIS, pg. 43; Image Source/OUP, pg. 46; © Rick Friedman/Corbis, pg. 47, © Tomohiro Ohsumi - Pool/ZUMA Press/Corbis, pg. 47; ABC-TV / The Kobal Collection / Zink, Vivian, pg. 49; © Klaus Tiedge/Corbis, pg. 50; Ocean/Corbis, pg. 51, Ryan Smith/Somos Images/Corbis, pg. 51, Skip Brown/Getty Image, pg. 51, YinYang/Getty Images, pg. 51; © Richard G. Bingham II / Alamy, pg. 52; Bruce Campbell, pg. 53; View Pictures/Peter Cook/VIEW/Newscom, pg. 54; © George Gutenberg/Beateworks/Corbis, pg. 55; baranq/Shutterstock, pg. 56; © KidStock/Blend Images/Corbis, pg. 59; Lionsgate / The Kobal Collection, pg. 60; © Sam Bloomberg-Rissman/Blend Images/Corbis, pg. 61; Martin Thomas Photography/Alamy, pg. 62; Caro / Alamy, pg. 63, Tetra Images/Corbis, pg. 63; Alex Livesey/Getty Images, pg. 64, Jim Kidd / Alamy, pg. 64, IS_ImageSource/Istock, pg. 64, Getty Images/Rich Lam, pg. 64; Getty Images/apixel, pg. 65; Minerva Studio/Shutterstock, pg. 67; Hayden Richard Verry/Alamy, pg. 68; Dave and Les Jacobs/Getty Images, pg. 69, udra11/shutterstock, pg. 69, Nejron Photo/Shutterstock, pg. 69, Andrew Watson/Alamy, pg. 69; OUP/Photodisc, pg. 70; rj lerich/Shuttertock, pg. 71; © Tim McGuire/Corbis, pg. 72; Chris Wilkinson/Alamy, pg. 73; Sam Bloomberg-Rissman/Blend Images/Corbis, back cover.